Hawaiian Flower Lei Making

Lei vendors near the Aloha Tower about 1920. (Hawaii State Archives photo.)

Hawaiian Flower Lei Making

Adren J Bird
and
Josephine Puninani Kanekoa Bird

A KOLOWALU BOOK • UNIVERSITY OF HAWAII PRESS • HONOLULU

© 1987 University of Hawai'i Press
All Rights Reserved
Printed in the United States of America
03 04 05 06 07 08   11 10 9 8 7 6

Library of Congress Cataloging-in-Publication Data

Bird, Adren J., 1926–
  Hawaiian flower lei making.

  (A Kolowalu book)
  Bibliography: p.
  1. Flower leis—Hawaii.   I. Bird, J. Puninani
Kanekoa (Josephine Puninani Kanekoa), 1926–
II. Title.
SB449.5.L4B57   1987   745.92'3   87-24347
ISBN 0-8248-1137-2

University of Hawai'i Press books are printed on
acid-free paper and meet the guidelines for permanence
and durability of the Council on Library Resources.

Printed by Data Reproductions Corporation

www.uhpress.hawaii.edu

This book is dedicated to our children, Kuuipo Grover, Kanekoa Bird, Anela Smith, Kealii Bird, and Mahina Bird, and to our thirteen grandchildren and one great-grandchild who all make up the jewels in our "Lei of Life."

CONTENTS

ACKNOWLEDGMENTS

Many people and several organizations helped in the preparation of this book. The authors gratefully acknowledge their generous assistance. Our mahalo nui is extended to the following individuals and organizations.

The Hawaii State Archives and the Brigham Young University-Hawaii Campus Archives provided photos which otherwise would be unavailable for our use. Donna Brown and the BYU-Hawaii farm furnished flowers and gave us advice on caring for flowers.

Debra McCoy and Dr. Margaret Baker provided assistance in reading and critiquing the manuscript as it progressed. Dr. Baker performed this service even though she was engaged in writing her doctoral dissertation at the time.

We thank Damaris A. Kirchhofer and the University of Hawaii Press editorial staff, without whose help this book would never have been produced.

We thank our children Jennifer Mahina Bird, Anela Smith, and Kuuipo Grover, who gave us constant encouragement and kokua when we needed it most, and our granddaughters Kuuipo Smith for helping us in weaving the crown flower leis and Puni Grover for modeling as a lei maker.

Last but not least, we give a special mahalo and aloha to Mitsuo Kajiwara for his generous gift of *maile* and *mokihana*. This gift required going into the mountains of Kauai, searching for the plants, and sending them to Oahu promptly. For this we are most grateful to Mitsuo and his daughter Paulette Akana, who coordinated the Kauai operation.

INTRODUCTION

Josephine Puninani Kanekoa Bird

Flower leis have been a part of my life for as long as I can remember. My mother and grandmother taught me as a child the Hawaiian names and characteristics of the flowers which grew abundantly along the Hana highway near Naihiku on the island of Maui. Scarcely a flower, leaf, or twig escaped our notice as we children walked along the highway with our *kuku* (grandmother) and at times with Mama and other relatives. We seldom missed a chance to try our hand at making leis when flowers were in season. It was not unusual for each of us to be wearing three or four flower leis of various kinds around our necks with *kukui* leaves tied about our heads as we walked between family dwellings. And if we were to visit an auntie, uncle, or cousin, extra leis were made to be shared once we arrived at their home. Leis made our day more pleasant and helped in keeping the love our family members had for one another alive and close. In a physical way, leis represented the *ALOHA* we felt in our hearts.

We children made certain that Mama nearly always had a lei to wear around the house. Many times we made leis for her and placed them around her neck as she prepared to attend church or other social events. My father was a county road supervisor. It was a normal occurrence for him to go to work wearing a flower lei on his hat, which had been fashioned by one or more of us from flowers and/or foliage growing in the yard.

At school leis were not an unusual sight, as children would make them on the way to school simply because the blossoms were so abundantly available along the roadside. Today people think there must be a special occasion when one is wearing a lei, but during my school years, no particular reason was needed to wear a lei. May Day, however, was a special day at school. Myriad leis were worn by everyone—children, teachers, and even the principal. Everyone competed in making the best lei they were capable of designing. Contests were held to select the most beautiful, the most innovative, and the most unusual leis for each grade level of schoolchildren.

Interestingly, before 1950, crepe paper leis were commonly worn, even when flowers were in season. During World War II, military personnel and other island visitors were given crepe paper leis more often than flower leis. When the Japanese-American 442nd Regimental Combat Team embarked for overseas, a crepe paper lei was presented to each of them individually by the people of

Hawaii. Flowers were not so abundant at the time, and the paper leis lasted longer. With patience and care, attractive paper and fabric leis can be made which last much longer than flower leis.

After my husband and I married, we moved to the mainland. Everywhere I went, people asked many questions about Hawaii and Hawaiian customs. One of the most frequent questions concerned flower leis and how to make them. I made many dandelion leis to demonstrate the principle of lei making and found, somewhat surprisingly, that dandelions can be formed into attractive *poepoe* leis. I also used carnations and roses to make *kui* leis, and I came to believe that with the right inspiration, a lei could be created from almost anything.

I remember well the February day in 1970 when our son was returning from Vietnam after two years, two wounds, and a Bronze Star. We were living in Provo, Utah, and I felt strongly that I must welcome my son home by presenting him with a lei when he arrived at the airport in Salt Lake City. But where would I ever get flowers on that blustery winter day? I asked my husband to stop at the grocery store and purchase two packages of chocolate candy kisses. Although he brought the candy without question, he was puzzled as to my purpose for getting it. I had a needle and thread and I began to string the wrapped candy as we traveled. By the time we arrived at the airport, I had made a lei for my son. I wasn't sure how he would receive it. To my surprise and pleasure, he was very happy and proud to be remembered in the "old Hawaiian way." This story is related to show that it is possible for a person with the desire to make a lei to do so in almost any circumstances, using the materials at hand and imagination.

This book provides illustrated, step-by-step instructions in basic lei-making techniques for several of the most common methods of lei construction. Beginning lei makers will be able to develop a solid foundation in lei-making skills and, perhaps, make their own contribution to the craft of lei making. It would be impossible to describe in a limited publication such as this the countless styles, methods, and creative variations of lei construction developed through the years. There are nearly as many different ways of constructing leis as there are people who make them. Therefore, the book is devoted to three basic kinds of floral leis:

1. The *kui* (needle) string lei, including the *kui pololei* (single), the *kui poepoe* (double), and the *kui lau* (leaf).
2. The *haku* lei, which is made by mounting flowers and/or other foliage against a natural base material such as dried banana leaf, ti leaf, or *lauhala*.
3. The *lau* (foliage) lei, including the *wili* (twisted) method, the *hili* (braided) method, and the *hīpu'u* (knotted) method.

We hope that this book will assist people everywhere to become proficient in lei-making skills, which can be used and enjoyed whenever a special expression of love, aloha, and honor is needed. Making and presenting a lei offers a way for the lei maker, wherever he or she happens to be, to participate in the preservation and growth of this beloved Hawaiian custom.

Chapter 1

The Lei

"A maile lei for your hair has a special meaning;
It's a sweet aloha made with love and care."
Norman Kaye

*T*hese lines express the affection and warmth of the Hawaiian lei. Hawaiians do not claim the distinction of originating the craft of lei making nor are they credited with any unusual ceremonies in connection with the practice of presenting leis. Some have claimed that in ancient times the *maile* lei was presented to Laka, the goddess of the *hula;* however, these accounts fall within the realm of mythology rather than recording any actual practices observed or reported about the early Hawaiians.

In the Hawaiian culture, a person's head and shoulders are considered sacred parts of the body, to be respected by others. Honoring those who are loved and respected has always been a fundamental value in Hawaii. It appears natural, when considering these cultural values, that the placing of a lei over the head and around the shoulders of a person would exemplify the bestowing of honor and respect. Native Hawaiians have demonstrated these values so sincerely that at least two words, *aloha* and *lei,*

have become universally known and used. Historically, leis have been a symbol of *"aloha"* for as long as the islands have been inhabited. The relationship of the two words is clearly seen when they are used together as a given name and in many sayings and song lyrics—*"lei aloha,"* or lei of love.

Adorning the human body with necklaces of shells, seeds, flowers, and foliage has been a custom in many parts of the world, including the Mediterranean, Asia, the Americas, and even northward into Scandinavia. Where flowers were scarce, many kinds of materials, including the bones and the skins of animals, were used in making necklaces to honor persons having distinguished themselves within their culture or according to national customs.

The ancient Israelites made leis of fruits in celebration of an abundant harvest. Fruits such as oranges, pomegranates and dates were tied or threaded together and draped over the shoulders of guests during harvest festi-

Flowing strands of crown flowers became the lei of preference in the late 1930s. (Hawaii State Archives photo.)

vals. The practice of threading fruits or flowers into leis to be used in celebration was later adopted in India and Southeast Asia.

In Hawaii, leis were made of feathers, foliage, and many other materials. The foliage leis were generally beautiful strings of fragrant *maile, ʻōlapa* leaves, or other vines *wili* (twisted) together and draped open-ended over the shoulders. Leis of fruits, seeds, human hair, and foliage are depicted in early paintings and drawings of Hawaii. Flower leis, however, are not noticeably present in these illustrations. Although the general use of floral leis before the arrival of the *haole* (foreigner) in the late eighteenth century cannot be verified, there is little doubt that flower leis were known to the Hawaiians, especially the *aliʻi* (royalty). Before the *haole* stepped ashore, however, there were few blossoms among the indigenous flowers that were suitable for lei making. Flower leis made by early Hawaiians most probably incorporated the *lehua, ʻilima,* and the blossoms of the *hou* tree, among other native flowers. Photographs taken around the turn of the twentieth century indicate that leis made of vines, with a relatively few blossoms woven into the open-ended garlands, were common. What is certain is that the Hawaiians possessed the skills for making many types of leis, demonstrated by the leis of shells, teeth, seeds, and feathers in various museum and other collections that predate the foreigner's arrival.

Modern Hawaiians have developed the craft of lei making to its highest point of artistry throughout the world. This was made possible through the numerous varieties of flowers brought into Hawaii in a relatively short period of time. Only a few flowers that are well known and commonly used for flower leis in present-day Hawaii were growing in the islands before 1850. Many people coming to the islands in the nineteenth century brought tropical and semitropical plants with them. Travelers and immigrants brought roses, violets, carnations, pansies, marigolds, jasmine *(pikake)*, gardenias, and plumeria (frangipani), among the many plants and flowers introduced after 1850. Cultivation of these foreign flowers made new floral materials available to Hawaiian lei makers to redesign and restructure the original Hawaiian lei. Many different styles and types of leis have been created since that time, and there is every reason to believe that new types of flower lei will continue to be designed as new varieties of flowers are introduced to the islands. Without the ingenuity and creative ability of the people native to these islands, however, Hawaiian leis would not have attracted the worldwide appeal and fame they now enjoy.

Ironically, tourism and commercialism have been largely responsible for the development and evolution of the Hawaiian craft of lei making. Sometime after 1870, enterprising Islanders commercialized the floral lei. Visitors to the islands admired the beautiful flowers that grew abundantly in the favorable subtropical climate. They were fascinated with the stringing and wearing of flower leis by Hawaiians. Leis were worn by the native Hawaiians on every occasion. There are reports of dockworkers, street cleaners, streetcar operators and schoolchildren wearing leis as a part of their everyday attire. Newcomers *(malihini)* gladly paid the lei vendor his price for the pleasure of wearing a flower lei. The reputations of individuals who were especially gifted in making

Departing passengers at the Aloha Tower about 1920. (BYU-Hawaii Archives.)

Lei vendors provided a choice between paper and flower leis about 1920. (Hawaii State Archives photo.)

the more attractive leis soon became known, and favorite lei makers were asked to supply floral leis for various occasions.

Between 1870 and the 1950s, passenger steamships and ocean liners called regularly at Honolulu. Lei vendors became a common sight along the harbor front near the Aloha Tower and on the docks, selling leis to both arriving and departing passengers. During these years, the custom of throwing leis over the ship's railing came into being. Some say it was done with the idea that if the lei thrown overboard drifted to the shore, the possessor of the lei would someday return to this island paradise. It is also reported that visitors felt it appropriate to return to the islands a portion of the *aloha* they had received during their stay. At any rate, many beautiful leis ended up in the waters of the harbor, thrown in by those who had received them as a gift of *aloha* shortly before the ship departed. Eventually, many departing passengers began to throw leis to friends on the dock below before the ship sailed. This resulted in many leis being trampled and strewn over the surface of the dock. The custom was discouraged and was finally discontinued with the decline of passenger ship service to the islands.

When the airplane replaced the ship as the preferred mode of transportation to and from Hawaii, lei vendors modernized their shops (including refrigeration) and

A ship's officer selects a flower lei from eager vendors about 1924. (Hawaii State Archives photo.)

Arriving passengers disembarking about 1924. Note the absence of paper or artificial leis. (BYU-Hawaii Archives.)

moved to locations near the major airports throughout the islands. The number of leis sold to tourists increased dramatically when air travel displaced the ocean liner. Ships would arrive once or twice a week with four or five hundred passengers. Airline arrivals occur every hour or so, bringing two to three hundred passengers with each arrival.

While the greatest number of lei vendors are located near transportation facilities, there are florists and lei shops in many shopping centers and business areas of Honolulu and other cities. Local people ordering leis for special occasions usually purchase them from shops that have lei makers talented in preparing special types of leis such as the cigar *(pua kika)*, *'ilima*, jasmine *(pikake)*, and the *maunaloa* style orchid lei.

Flower leis are enjoyed by local people as well as visitors to the islands. For example, it is awe-inspiring to anyone attending a commencement or graduation ceremony in Hawaii for the first time to see the huge number of leis presented to each graduate. Recipients are often obliged to carry some of them on their arms when the number of leis placed around their necks reaches eye level.

Weddings, birthday parties, graduations, and retirement celebrations; parades, May Day, Kamehameha Day, political rallies, and many other occasions are all marked by the abundance of flower leis worn by participants or those being honored. At the opening of the Hawaii State Legislature each year mountains of leis are presented to the lawmakers and their assistants. Not only the legislators but everyone in attendance wears at least one flower lei. The giving of leis, the singing of Hawaiian songs, and the general good will among the participants contribute

By the 1930s both clothing styles and lei construction had changed. (Hawaii State Archives photo.)

Mahina Bird and her friend Wendy at their high school graduation.

King Kamehameha's statue draped with leis during annual Kamehameha Day festivities. (Photo courtesy of Jim Kirchhofer.)

to a wonderful *aloha* spirit, which makes the opening session a unique and remarkable experience among all state legislatures.

Many of the modifications in modern lei making have come about through friendly competition. Perhaps no other people love the spirit of competition quite as much as native Hawaiians. The grandest part of any competition is to create a "secret" design or innovation that will inspire awe and envious admiration from others. It is not unusual for a Hawaiian *'ohana* (family) to develop a new method of making or preparing an item, such as a lei, and keep it secret until a contest for such items is held. Lei makers have the chance to unveil their latest creations each year when the City and County of Honolulu Department of Parks and Recreation sponsors the largest lei contest in the state. Any lei maker who designs and constructs a lei that meets its rather stringent rules may enter the contest, where the leis are judged by experts in the field. It is interesting to note that this love of competition has been responsible not only for the development of a rich variety of lei styles but also for the revival of ancient dances (the Merry Monarch Hula Festival, for example), the writing of songs and music (the Hoku Awards for best song, composer, recording star), and many other crafts and skills associated with Hawaiian culture.

At least two rules of etiquette apply concerning the giving and receiving of leis. First, the giving of a lei is a token of love and esteem. When a lei is made with a particular person in mind, it should never be worn before it is given to that person. As with any gift, one would not use the gift before presenting it to the individual for whom it was intended. Second, the manner in which a lei is received also displays the love and appreciation the recipient has for the giver. Therefore, a lei is always received with a kiss and an embrace.

The mastery of lei making must be preserved as well as refined. As with all art, it is a growing, developing practice that must not become stale nor be allowed to die. The perpetuation of the skills necessary to continue the tradition and to improve the methods of constructing leis is the responsibility of those who understand and have a love for this custom. It is for this reason that every pattern, style, and type of lei should be considered a valid contribution to this ageless and continually developing art.

A prize-winning *lei haku* at the City and County of Honolulu's May Day lei contest.

Chapter 2

The *Lei Kui* or String Lei

*P*erhaps the easiest and most common style of lei produced in Hawaii is the string lei or *lei kui*. Once the technique is learned, a *lei kui* can be made rather quickly with many different types of blossoms in the straight *(pololei)* or round *(poepoe)* style. However, the simplicity of construction should not tempt the lei maker into producing a lei of any less quality than would be achieved if a more complex style were used. The string lei can be most beautiful and appealing if made with care and practiced skill.

Making a lei requires some understanding of the basic tools and materials used. Beyond that, the stringing is mostly a matter of personal preference as to the appearance of the finished product. There are many blossoms and other plant materials that can be strung into a lei. (Appendix 1 contains a list of suggested flowers for the *kui pololei* or *poepoe*.) It is the method used to assemble a lei as well as the flowers and other materials that put the lei maker's signature on the work. Prominent lei makers' work can be recognized by the quality and style of the workmanship and the choice of materials used in constructing the lei.

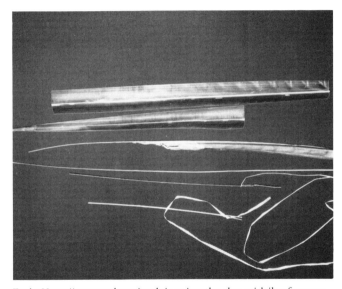

Early Hawaiians made string leis using the dry midrib of a coconut leaf *(nī'au)*. The midrib was prepared by removing all of the leaf material and smoothing the midrib with the fingers or a rough cloth. The point was sharpened and a notch was cut near the base end to hold the stringing material.

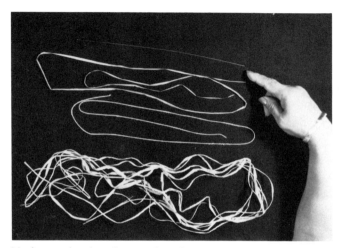

Modern technology has produced a steel needle for stringing leis. These needles vary in length from about 12 to 18 inches. Raffia, *hau* bark fiber, and other natural stringy material can be used with the steel needles as well as modern types of string or thread.

The *lei kui* was first made in Hawaii using the *nī'au,* the midrib of a coconut leaf, as a needle to pull the string through the flowers. *Nī'au* are prepared by cleaning all traces of the leaf from a dry midrib about 12 inches in length, sharpening the pointed tip, and cutting a small notch to secure the string in the base end. The *nī'au* can be used even today and, in fact, is preferred by some lei makers. However, steel needles especially designed for making leis are available and can be purchased from novelty and variety stores. These needles, which vary in length from 12 to 18 inches, are popular with professional lei makers because of their sharpness, strength, and small diameter.

The fibrous bark of the *hau* tree *(Hibiscus tiliaceus),* banana fiber, and other natural stringy materials may be used as thread. Dental floss, raffia, polished twine, thread (waxed or regular), common string, strips of fabric, and even strips of flexible plastic can also be used in making the *lei kui*. The durability and frailty of the blossoms being strung and the availability of materials should determine what is used to string the lei. Whatever threading material is used, it is important that it be long enough to make the lei an appropriate length without having to knot the thread to increase the lei's length.

We recommend carpet thread or No. 10 cotton thread for stringing most *kui* type leis; these threads are readily available and strong enough to resist breaking with normal wear and use of the lei. If finer threads than these are used there is a tendency for the thread to cut and tear the blossoms when the lei is worn. When delicate blossoms are used in constructing a lei, waxed thread of various weights is recommended.

In order to have firm, crisp blossoms to work with, the flowers should be picked in the early morning. It is essential for the blossoms to hold their shape until the lei can be made and presented to the person for whom it is intended. Some blossoms can be refrigerated before or after making the lei. Others, such as *pua kenikeni,* keep better when stored on a damp cloth in subdued light. (See Appendix 2 for care of flowers.)

In selecting flowers suitable for leis, the lei maker should be aware of any disadvantages the plant may present. There are some important considerations in selecting materials that apply to any type of lei.

1. The fragrance of the flower or plant: It is important that materials selected do not have an unpleasant scent. Flowers with no fragrance are a better choice for lei making than those with an unpleasant odor.

2. The durability of the flower should be such that it will keep its shape and fragrance for a reasonable length of time—a day or two is generally sufficient. After all, flowers begin to wilt the moment they are picked. Some will last longer than others, but the most beautiful and fragrant flowers give their "aloha" for only a day—two at the most. When proper care is given to the lei, it may be kept presentable for a couple of days.

3. Flowers should not be poisonous or irritating to the skin. The *mokihana,* for example, is desirable for use in leis because of its pleasing scent, which lasts long after the seed has wilted and turned from green to dark grey in color. However, some people are sensitive to the *mokihana* seed pods; therefore, direct contact with the skin should be avoided. The *mokihana* lei is often used in combination with other foliage using the *wili* or *haku*

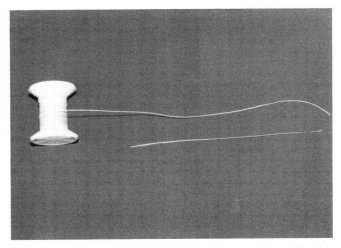

For general all-purpose lei making, No. 10 cotton thread should be used. The thread is readily available and is strong enough to resist breaking during normal wearing of a lei. This size thread also fits the steel lei needle without difficulty.

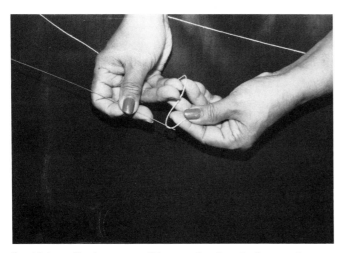

Steel lei needles have a small loop or hook at the base end which holds the thread yet allows the needle to pass through the blossoms without tearing them. The loop at the base of these needles will accommodate No. 10 cotton or waxed carpet thread. Thread the needle as shown.

style in order to minimize contact with the skin. The milky sap discharged from the crown flower bush and the plumeria tree are poisonous and irritating to the skin and eyes. Caution should be used when preparing these flowers for leis.

4. The blossoms or combination of flowers should lend themselves to a neat and orderly design. The colors should be in harmony, complementing and forming a well-planned and interesting pattern.

5. The weight of the finished lei is an important consideration. If the lei weighs more than 8 to 10 ounces (lighter for small people or children) it will soon become uncomfortable to the wearer.

6. The flowers selected should be available in good supply, ample for completing the number of leis desired. Also, blossoms that are scarce may be too expensive for the lei maker to finish the lei as it should be. When foliage and flowers are taken from the wild, it is important to gather only what is needed and give nature a chance to replace what was taken.

The yellow plumeria and the multicolored carnation are commonly used in making string leis commercially and for personal use. In recent years, the orchid, especially the vanda variety, has become very popular because of its versatility. It is used in making both the single strand *(kui pololei)* and the *maunaloa* style leis. Other flowers used frequently are the crown flower, the tuberose *(Polianthes tuberosa)*, various species of bougainvillea, and the *pua kenikeni*. These flowers have the advantage of being sturdy enough to withstand relatively rough handling and have a natural structure which allows the worker to make leis of different styles. There are many other flowers that can be used, giving the lei maker a large assortment to choose from and great variety to create a beautiful work of art—the Hawaiian flower lei.

PLUMERIA

One of the most common straight or single string leis *(kui pololei)* is made with plumeria blossoms (*Plumeria* spp.) Plumeria is usually available from early spring to late fall. Most varieties can withstand somewhat rougher handling than other blossoms. The blossoms are easily gathered, cleaned, and strung, which presents an advantage when a lei is needed in a hurry. In the latter part of the nineteenth century and into the early twentieth century, when people died in Hawaii they were not embalmed, as a general rule, which necessitated their burial on the same day that death occurred or, at the latest, the following day. Because funerals were held soon after death, relatives and friends rushing to attend the services would gather any available flowers for leis and wreaths. Usually many more plumeria leis were presented at these quickly arranged funerals than leis made with other blossoms because of their availability and ease in stringing. For this reason, the blossom earned the undeserved title of "*make*-man" or dead-man flower.

The many varieties of the plumeria have become commercialized to such a high degree that nearly all persons in the islands, residents as well as visitors, have enjoyed a lei of this sweetly scented flower at some time or other. The yellow plumeria lei is the most widely made and distributed flower lei in Hawaii. Therefore, it seems appropriate to begin the instructions with the making of this ever-popular lei.

These young hula dancers are wearing plumeria leis.

Step 1. When preparing the blossoms for threading, carefully sort them according to size and color. This step is necessary to produce a uniform lei. A minimum of 50 large yellow plumeria blossoms is needed for a good size lei. However, if the flowers are of different sizes, large and small blossoms may be used alternately; in this case it will take 75 to 100 flowers. The length of the lei will vary with the size of the person for whom it is intended. Usually a 40-inch lei is sufficient; however, it can be as long as the lei maker wishes. As a good rule of thumb, the lei should reach the bottom of the person's ribcage when hanging directly from the neck.

Step 2. To begin stringing the lei, hold the blossom by the stem with the face of the flower toward you. Insert the needle into the corolla tube (the tube running through the flower), and push the needle completely through the blossom. Each blossom should be placed on the needle in the same manner.

Step 3. Continue adding blossoms to the needle. After 5 to 8 flowers have been placed on the needle, gently push the group of blossoms from the needle onto the thread.

Step 4. Although it is not necessary at this point to be concerned about the position of the blossoms on the string, as the lei is constructed the blossoms will gradually work themselves toward the end of the string.

Step 5. Continue adding flowers as described in steps 2 and 3 until the length of thread is filled with blossoms. Leave at least 1½ inches of thread at each end.

Step 6. The lei is completed by pulling the flowers closely together, not too tightly but firmly enough to hold the shape of the lei, and tying the two ends of the thread together. Tie a satin ribbon bow (or some other appropriate bow) at the point of the lei where the ends of the thread are joined.

PUA KENIKENI

The *pua kenikeni (Fagraea berteriana),* or ten cent flower, provides a fragrant and colorful single or double strand lei. This flower was called simply the *pua* flower when it was first brought to Hawaii from the South Pacific. However, Hawaiians soon named it the *pua keni-keni* because the blossoms sold for ten cents each. When this flower is ready to pick, it is a creamy white color. After it is picked the blossom gradually changes from creamy white to yellow, then to an orange shade, and finally to a brown color. The fragrance will last even after the flower has withered and turned light brown.

The flower is picked from the shrub or tree by breaking the stem. This leaves the calyx (the green, leafy base) on the blossom. A *pua kenikeni pololei* of 40 to 52 inches will require about 50 to 70 blossoms. This lei may be strung on a narrow strip of cotton material or knitting yarn; string or thread may cut through the blossom because of the large diameter of the corolla tube.

Step 1. In order to string the lei, the calyx must be removed. Use a pair of scissors to cut the blossom at right angles to the corolla tube about half the distance between the calyx and the petals. If blossoms are in short supply, the flower may be cut close to the stem end in order to retain the long corolla tube and thereby reduce the number of blossoms needed for the lei.

Step 2. After cutting the blossoms to the appropriate length, begin stringing the lei. Hold the blossom by the stem end, insert the needle into the tube from the petal end, and push the needle through the tube.

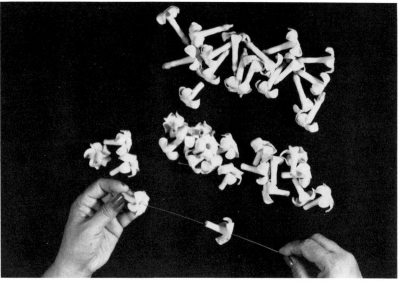

Step 3. Continue placing blossoms on the needle in this manner until there are 5 to 8 blossoms on the needle.

Step 4. Gently push the blossoms from the needle onto the thread. Repeat the operation by placing more blossoms on the needle and transferring them to the thread.

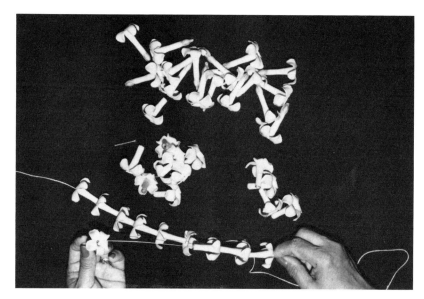

Step 5. When enough blossoms have been placed on the string or yarn to complete a lei of an appropriate length, cut the yarn, leaving about an inch and a half on each end for tying the yarn ends together. Complete the lei by placing a bow tied from ribbon in a complementary color where the yarn has been tied together.

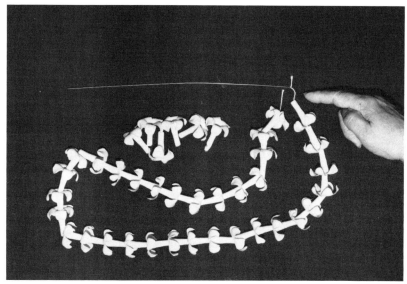

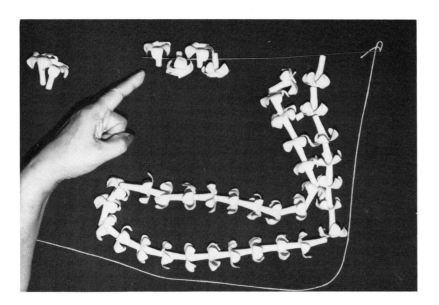

Pua Kenikeni, Poepoe Style

Step 1. The *pua kenikeni* may also be strung by cutting off the stems closer to the petal end and pushing the needle crosswise through the corolla tube. This round or "double" lei is called *kui poepoe,* and 150 to 200 blossoms will be required to complete a lei in this style.

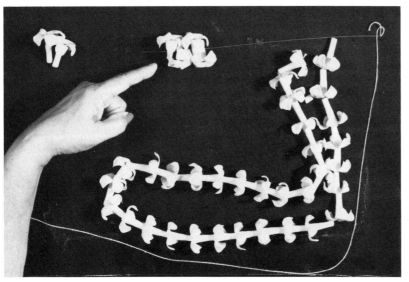

Step 2. By pushing the blossoms together, the petals of one flower cover the open stem end of the other. This makes a beautiful lei. The lei maker should be aware that this style requires at least four times the number of blossoms needed for the straight or single lei *(kui pololei)* because the blossoms will face outward in at least four different directions.

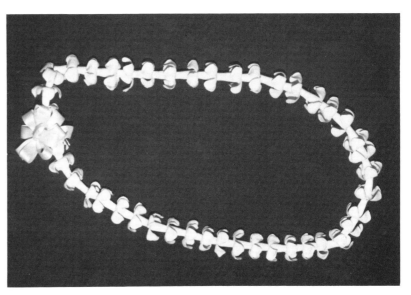

The *pua kenikeni* in the *kui pololei* style (top) and in the *kui poepoe* style.

VANDA ORCHID

The vanda orchid *(Vanda Miss Joaquim)* has become one of the most favored and versatile flowers for leis. Although, like most orchids, it has no fragrance, the vanda can be used to make at least four distinct styles of lei. Unless the wearer is familiar with the blossom, the leis made in these styles appear to be made from four different blossoms. One side of the vanda is a darker shade of lavender than the other. The blossom can be separated very easily into two parts, one part having a color distinct from the other, which makes it possible to construct the different lei styles.

Single Vanda Lei

Step 1. Using about 50 to 60 blossoms, string the vanda just as you would any other blossom to make a single *lei kui*. Place the needle at the crown of the calyx (the prominent pale-colored point in the middle of the blossom) and push the needle through the stem end of the flower.

Step 2. Continue adding blossoms to the needle and transfer them to the thread until the lei is at least 40 inches in length. Leave 1 1/2 inches of thread at each end and tie the thread together to complete the single vanda lei.

Maunaloa Style Vanda Lei

The darker part of the vanda blossom can be used to create the *maunaloa*-style lei. The true *maunaloa* flower
(Canavalia microcarpa) grows on a vine throughout the
islands. The *maunaloa* is related to the pea family and
cannot be exported because of a virus it carries. However, the vanda orchid has been used to develop a lei
style similar to the lei made from the true *maunaloa*
flower. In fact, the similarities are such that the name
maunaloa is commonly used to describe this kind of lei
made from vanda orchid blossoms. Also, since the vanda
is cultivated for lei making, it is much more plentiful and
is in season for a longer part of the year than the true
maunaloa flower.

The *maunaloa* style vanda lei requires from 150 to
200 blossoms in order to produce a well-balanced, full-
length lei (approximately 40 inches). It is made with the
darker side of the blossom. The two parts of the vanda
blossom are not only different in color but have distinct
shapes, which make them appear, when separated, to be
two totally different flowers.

The preparation of a *maunaloa* lei during the mid-1930s.
(Hawaii State Archives photo.)

Step 1. Taking the dark side of the blossom between the thumb and forefinger of one hand and the lighter side of the blossom in like manner with the other hand, *gently* twist and pull until the blossom breaks in half. Break about 200 blossoms in half, or until you have enough to complete the number of leis desired.

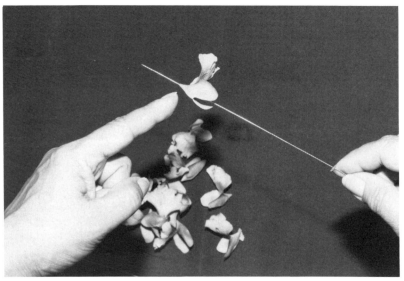

Step 2. While holding the dark part of the blossom, insert the needle between the two firm lips forming the dark half of the flower. The needle should exit at the apex of the slightly yellow center tip of the flower.

Step 3. Hold the next blossom so that the soft petal connected to this part of the flower extends to the opposite side of the needle. Push the needle between the two firm lips of the flower and through the center of the blossom.

Step 4. Push the two blossom halves together so that the two firm lips of the last blossom placed on the needle overlap the lips of the first blossom. This should be done with reasonable care to avoid bruising or otherwise damaging the flowers.

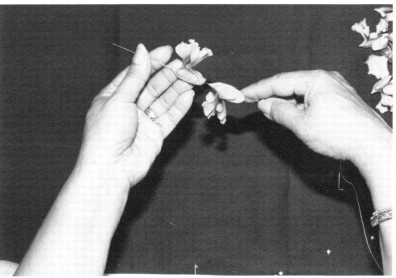

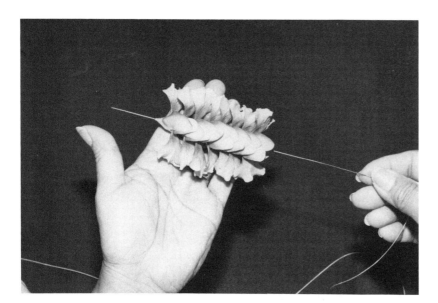

Step 5. Continue adding blossom halves, alternating the loose or fluffy petal from one side of the needle to the other with the firm lips of the blossoms overlapping those previously place on the needle. The fluffy petals will lie to both sides of the firm center and point in opposite directions. Construct the lei in sections while the blossoms are still on the needle in order to see how the finished product will take shape.

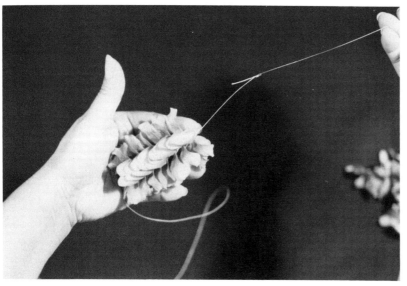

Step 6. With this style lei, the transfer of the blossoms from the needle to the thread must be done carefully with only a few blossoms at a time. Slide the sections or groups of blossoms onto the thread, making sure the overlap of the firm lips of the blossom is uniform. It is essential that the overlapping lips are held firmly in place. Pull the thread relatively tight before tying, leaving no slack for spaces to develop between the overlapping lips as the lei is worn. Leave an inch and a half of thread at each end for tying the lei. Add a ribbon bow to complete the lei.

The Half *Maunaloa* (Centipede Style) Vanda Lei

There is an especially attractive variation of the vanda *maunaloa* style developed within the past few years that has a fascinating appearance. This was first called the "centipede" style. However, because of the negative connotation of the word "centipede," most lei vendors prefer to call it the "half *maunaloa*" vanda lei. This lei will require about the same number of blossoms needed to construct the *maunaloa* (about 200). Only the darker half of the blossoms is used for this style lei.

Step 1. Select and prepare the vanda blossoms by breaking them in half in the same manner required to construct the *maunaloa* style vanda lei.

Step 2. After a sufficient number of blossoms have been prepared separate the two halves of the blossoms. (Save the lighter colored petals to make another type of vanda lei.) Begin placing the petals on the needle by piercing the calyx and pushing the needle down the stem of the blossom.

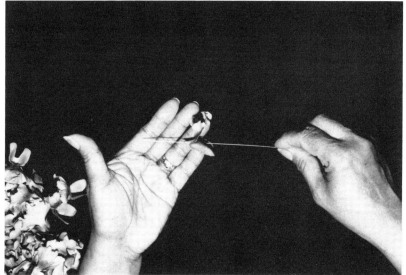

Step 3. The needle should be inserted into the open end of the flower formed by the two firm lips of the blossom. The needle should emerge through the pale yellow ovary end of the blossom.

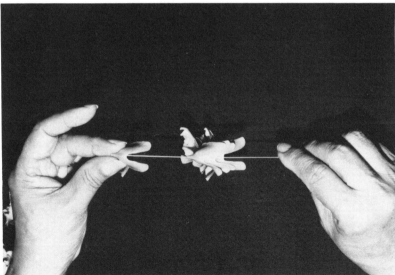

Step 4. All the blossoms are placed on the needle in the same way, allowing the firm lips of the blossoms to overlap when they are brought together while the fluffy petals extend to one side of the lei only.

This photo shows the effect of extending the fluffy petals to one side while the firm lips of the blossoms overlap on the other side.

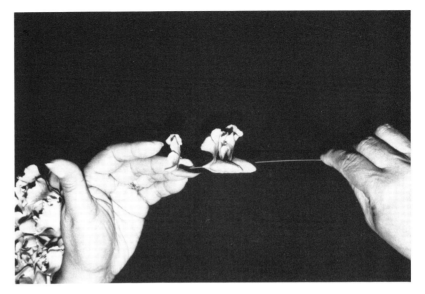

Step 5. Continue to place blossoms on the needle until there are 8 to 10 aligned, as illustrated.

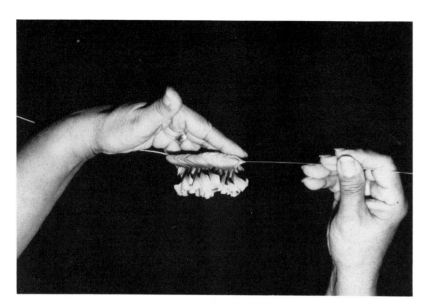

Step 6. Gently, but firmly, grasp the blossoms by the overlapping lip portion of the cluster.

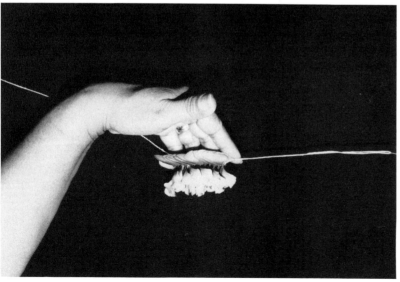

Step 7. While grasping the cluster of blossoms, pull them from the needle to the thread. Keep the cluster intact as it moves onto the thread in order to reduce the amount of rearranging necessary as the lei progresses.

Step 8. Continue to place petals on the needle one at a time, building a cluster of blossoms arranged in the proper manner, and gently transfer the cluster from the needle to the thread.

Step 9. As each new cluster is placed on the thread, pull it snugly against the clusters already transferred, taking care that the firm lips of the first blossom of the cluster being moved to the thread overlap those of the last blossom of the preceding cluster.

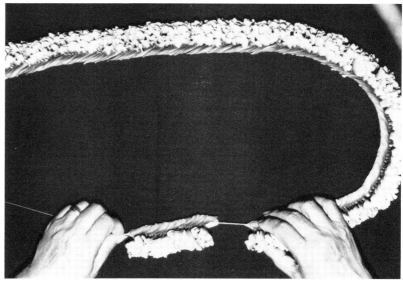

Step 10. To finish the lei, pull the ends of the string together firmly. The petals at each end will fit into one another. Tie the ends of the string together with a square knot, carefully pulling the knot down into the petals so it is hidden from view. Trim the loose ends of the thread.

Step 11. Tie a ribbon at the point where the ends of the string have been tied. This completes the lei.

Using Light-Colored Vanda Petals

The light-colored halves of the vanda blossom that are not used when a *maunaloa* lei is made can be discarded or used to string a lei which has a beauty of its own. The petals may be strung in a *kui lau* (leaf lei) style. The petals on this part of the blossom are so delicate that the lei will seldom last more than one or two days, even when the lei is well cared for. You will need 150 or more blossoms.

Step 1. After the vanda blossoms have been separated, collect the light-colored petals and prepare a needle and thread to begin stringing.

Step 2. Begin stringing the lei by pushing the needle through the stamen portion of the petal.

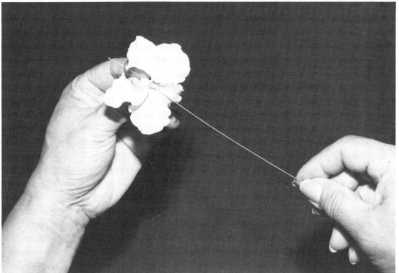

Step 3. After the needle has been pushed through the petal, align the petal on the needle and pierce another, which will overlap the first blossom.

Step 4. The petals are very delicate; therefore, it is a good idea to transfer a small number (4 or 5) at a time from the needle to the thread.

Step 5. Continue piercing the petals with the needle and transferring them onto the thread until the desired length for the lei has been reached. Leave enough thread to tie the lei. Place a ribbon at the knot in the thread and lei is complete.

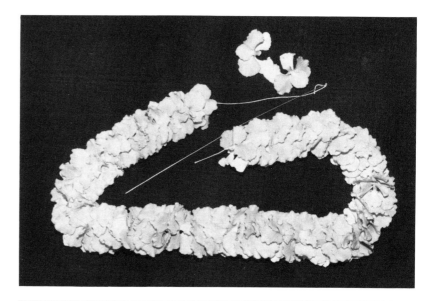

The *maunaloa* style lei and the lei made from the light-colored petals are approximately the same length when 150 or more blossoms are used. The appearance of vanda leis made in the two styles is markedly different.

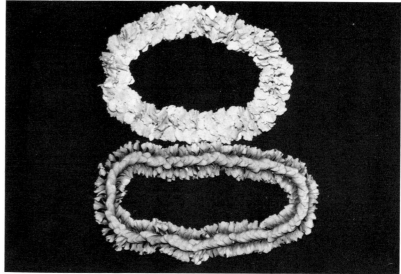

HALA

The fruit of the *hala* tree or screw pine *(Pandanus odoratissimus)*, also called pandanus, has long been used for the making of leis by the Hawaiians—indeed, it is a lei found throughout Polynesia. The fruit grows on the female tree at the end of the branches. Each fruit grows in a spherical shape from 8 to 10 inches in diameter, the outer covering resembling that of a pineapple. However, the segments or keys grow individually, each being attached to the core of the fruit. As they ripen, each key will fall independently from the core.

There are numerous ways to style a lei from *hala,* but only one method will be demonstrated here. This is the *lei hala* made with pieces of *laua'e (Microsorium scolopendria),* a fragrant fern, inserted between each key or segment. The individual keys used to make *hala* leis may vary from a pale yellow to a crimson red, depending upon the variety of pandanus used. There are at least twenty-three different varieties of pandanus in Hawaii.

According to Hawaiian custom, a *lei hala* is a gift of love and best wishes to be given upon the arrival of a friend or visitor. Custom dictates that giving a *lei hala* to someone beginning a new business or one who is going away is in poor taste. It is said that the *hala* brings bad luck to a new business, and when a person is departing, the gift of a *lei hala* carries a wish that the giver and the receiver may never meet again!

When you make a *lei hala* for yourself, however, no one can be offended. And indeed, the *lei hala* is a popular and traditional lei that is also very beautiful, whatever style is used.

One good-sized *hala* fruit will yield enough keys for one, and perhaps two, leis.

Hala leis are sometimes constructed by stringing together only the cut keys. The keys should be cut carefully so they fit against one another without showing the thread or other stringing material used in making the lei. By adding pieces of a strong green leaf, such as the *laua'e* fern, between each segment, however, the beauty of the lei is greatly enhanced.

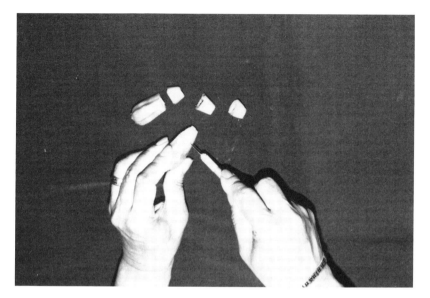

Step 1. Only the soft end of each key is used in making the lei. The outer end, the seed end, is discarded. Trim each key with a sharp knife (an X-acto knife is ideal). The keys may be cut straight across as shown.

Step 2. As an alternative to the straight cut, several small cuts may be made at about a 30 degree angle toward the center of the key. The cuts should not go deeper than the center of the key. When the carving is completed, the key will have several points around a small depression, which allows each key to fit snugly onto the end of the key preceding it when the lei is strung.

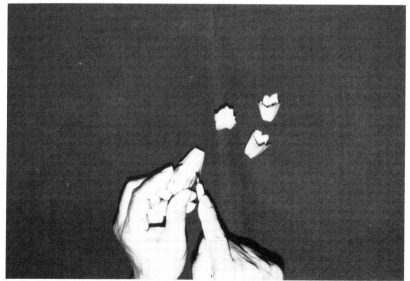

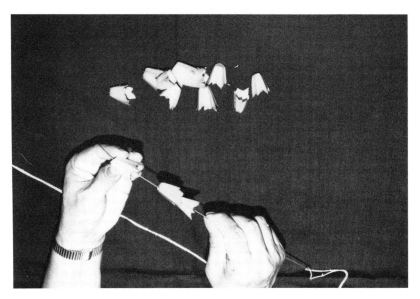

Step 3. The keys are strung by pushing the lei needle through the length of each. The thread should pass through the key parallel to the grain of its fiber.

Step 4. The *laua'e* is a popular and sturdy fern used commonly with *hala*. As the *laua'e* matures, small seeds grow in the leaf itself. For making a *lei hala* chose *laua'e* leaves that do not have seeds.

Step 5. Use a pair of sharp scissors or a sharp knife on a hard surface to cut the *laua'e* to the desired shape and size. Leaf pieces should be large enough to extend beyond the *hala,* so that the green color accentuates the yellow or red of the *hala.*

Step 6. Begin the lei by pushing the lei needle longitudinally, with the grain of the fiber, through the key.

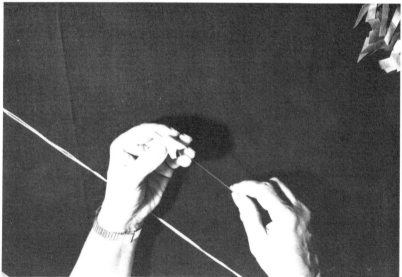

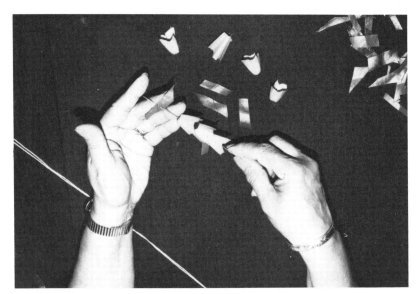

Step 7. Add a piece or two of *laua'e* leaf after the key is on the needle. The next key is followed by more pieces of *laua'e* leaf. This process is continued until enough keys and pieces of *laua'e* leaf have been added to make the lei an appropriate length.

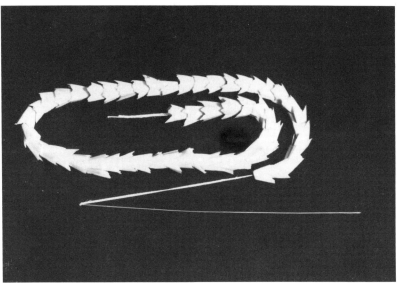

This is a plain *lei hala* made from cut key segments only.

This is a *lei hala* made with cut sections of *laua'e* inserted between each key segment.

The traditional *lei hala* makes an especially nice gift for family and friends. It will always be well received by people familiar with Polynesian cultures.

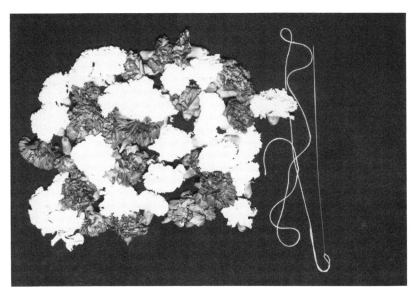

Red and white blossoms are used to make the single carnation lei described here.

CARNATION

Missionary wives are credited with bringing the carnation (*Dianthus caryophyllus* L.) to Hawaii sometime between 1840 and 1870. The first variety of carnation brought to the islands was a white, scented flower, which soon became a favorite with both lei makers and those wearing leis made with its blossoms. Red carnations were introduced sometime later. When it was discovered that white carnations placed in water containing various shades of food coloring would absorb the color, multicolored carnation leis became fashionable. Soon green, blue, yellow, and carnations in other tints were being made into leis. A variety of pink carnation was also imported and it too became popular as a lei flower.

The carnation may be used in combination with other flowers, such as tuberose, rosebuds, vanda or dendrobium orchids, and plumeria, to name a few of the most common combinations. The only caution to be exercised when using the carnation with other flowers is in selecting a flower whose color will complement that of the carnation. The lei can be strung as a single blossom lei *(pololei)* or as a double blossom lei *(poepoe)* when the calyx (the green, leafy base of the blossom) is removed or split.

Single Carnation Lei

To complete a single carnation lei, a total of 40 to 60 blossoms will be needed. Blossoms of different colors may be alternated in making a carnation lei. Select a length of string, *hau* fiber, or raffia sufficient for the appropriate length lei. Use a long steel lei needle.

Step 1. Run the needle through the blossom from the center of the petals through the center of the stem end. The stems should be cut close to the calyx, leaving little or no stem on each blossom.

The needle should exit the blossom as near the center of the stem as possible so that the blossoms may be drawn close together to insure that the lei will lay straight when worn.

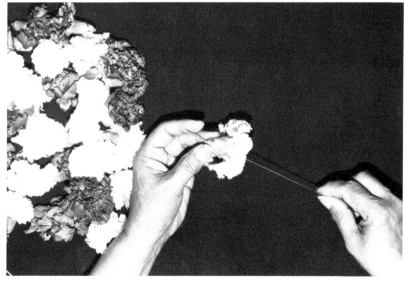

Step 2. If blossoms of different colors are being used, select another color blossom and push the needle through the flower the same way.

Step 3. Continue adding different color blossoms alternately to the needle until a set of four or five carnations is on the needle.

Step 4. Transfer the blossoms to the string by pulling them as a group from the needle onto the string. Continue piercing blossoms with the lei needle and moving them onto the string. Be sure that the color pattern remains the same.

Step 5. Once a sufficient number of blossoms has been placed on the string to provide an appropriate length (approximately 40 inches), remove the needle from the string and tie the ends together, pulling the blossoms rather snugly together. A ribbon should be added to the lei at the point where the ends of the string have been tied. This completes the lei.

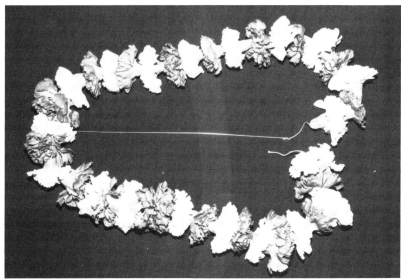

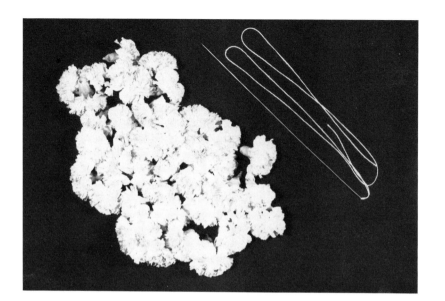

Double Carnation Lei

A double carnation lei is usually made using blossoms of one color. One hundred twenty-five to 170 blossoms are needed for this lei. No. 10 thread may be used as well as the other stringing materials previously mentioned. Use a long steel lei needle.

Step 1. The calyx of each blossom must be removed or split open in order to construct this style lei. Grasp the petal part of the blossom, holding it firmly.

Step 2. While holding the petals with one hand, peel the leaves of the calyx from the blossom.

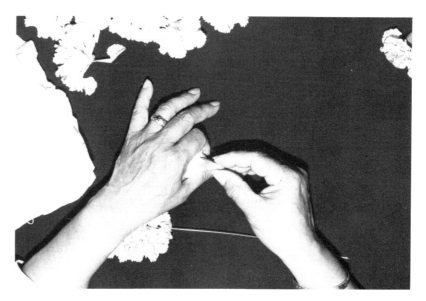

Step 3. The blossom will have to be rotated if the calyx is to be removed entirely from each part of the blossom. It is best to remove the calyx leaves from all the blossoms you intend to use for the lei before beginning the stringing. This gives you the opportunity to select the best blossoms and to complete the stringing operation without interruption.

Step 4. Once the calyx leaves have been removed, the petals will become very loose and will appear so fragile that it will seem as though the blossom will fall apart. However, the petals are still held firmly around the ovary area of the blossom and will spread out more fully.

Step 5. Insert the lei needle horizontally through the ovary area of the blossom. (The string should be long enough to avoid having to lengthen it during the stringing.)

Step 6. Blossoms should be bunched on the needle in groups of 3 to 6.

Step 7. Rotate the blossoms on the needle to form the desired round *(poepoe)* pattern. In making this style lei, the blossoms will face outward from the string rather than up and down.

As more blossoms are added to the needle, continue rotating the flowers and aligning them in the round pattern.

Step 8. Transfer the blossoms to the string in groups, keeping the round pattern that is distinctive of the double carnation lei. Continue this procedure until the lei has sufficient blossoms to bring it to the desired length (from 36 to 40 inches).

Step 9. Tie the ends of the string together, keeping the flowers firmly packed together. The ends of the string should be trimmed and hidden within the blossoms.

Step 10. To complete the lei, tie a bow to the lei at the point where the string ends are tied.

A typical cluster of crown flowers showing the blossoms and buds in various stages of development.

CROWN FLOWER

The lavender crown flower *(Calotropis gigantea)* first appeared in Hawaii about 1890. Called *pua kalaunu* by Hawaiians, it was a favorite of Queen Lili'uokalani. She loved the faint fragrance of the flower and its sturdiness, which allowed leis made from it to be used for two or three days with a minimum of care. The flower's unique aroma is light and does not offend one's sense of smell.

The crown flower grows on a large bush with abundant clusters of blossoms at the ends of each branch. Each cluster consists of fully opened flowers and buds in various stages of bloom. The petals of the older blossoms curl under the flower toward the stem, leaving the "crown" of the flower protruding outward from the petals.

The thick, white gummy sap which exudes from the stem and branch of the crown flower when cut is poisonous. It should never be tasted or taken internally. Some people are sensitive to this sap, and it should be removed from the skin as soon as possible.

Several different leis can be made from the crown flower using the blossoms in various stages of development and also by using different parts of the flower. The buds, petals, and crown of the flower may be used separately, as well as the entire blossom. The segments of the crown can even be separated and meticulously strung as a unique and beautiful lei. Four types of crown flower lei will be demonstrated here.

Crowns

Seventy to 80 crowns are required for a strand of crown flowers using the crowns only. Since three or four strands of crown flowers are usually worn together, it is recommended that 150 to 300 crowns be separated before you begin stringing the lei.

Separate the blossoms and the buds. Also separate the older blossoms with curled petals from the younger, fully opened blossoms.

Step 1. Using the mature blossoms, break the crown from each blossom. (The crowns from young, fully opened flowers may also be used if you want to keep the petals for making other leis.)

Step 2. Remove the crowns from the petals by grasping the crown in one hand and the petals in the other. Twist the two parts of the flower in opposite directions and they will separate quite easily. The separation should be done carefully, if the petals are to be used for another lei.

Step 3. Using the steel lei needle, begin by piercing the crown from the top, with the needle emerging at the stem end.

Step 4. Place 6 to 8 crowns on the needle in a uniform manner.

Step 5. Transfer the crowns to the thread or string and continue to *kui* the lei using the same technique as before.

Step 6. A single strand constitutes a crown flower lei. However, you may want to combine several strands together to make the lei more supple and full. The number of strands is determined by individual taste. Tie the ends together to complete a multistrand lei.

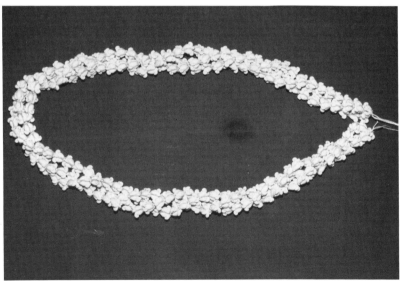

Step 7. Several strands may also be twisted *(wili)* for a different and impressive effect. Whichever way you decide to finish the lei, simply tie the strings together, trim the loose ends, and add a bow of an appropriate color at the point where the strings have been tied.

Whole Crown Flower Lei

When using the entire crown flower blossom for a lei, select the best of the newly opened and fully developed blossoms. This lei requires from 50 to 70 blossoms, with petals. A better-looking lei can be made if the blossoms are uniform in color and shape.

Step 1. Pierce the flower with the needle from the top of the crown through to the stem end of the blossom. Place 3 to 5 flowers on the needle in a uniform design.

Step 2. Transfer the blossoms from the needle to the string by holding the needle with one hand and gently pulling the blossoms from the needle onto the string.

Step 3. Continue to place flowers on the string in the manner just described until a lei of the desired length has been made.

Step 4. As the blossoms are transferred from the needle to the string, they should be pulled against one another tightly until the string is filled with flowers.

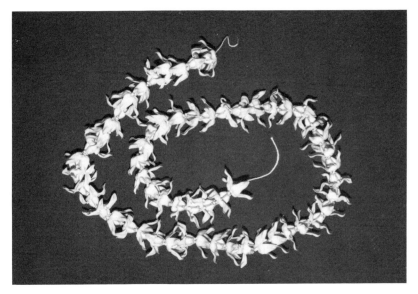

Step 5. Pull the blossoms snugly together and tie the ends of the string together. Trim the loose ends of the string and tie a ribbon on the lei at the point where the ends have been connected.

Crown Flower Petal Lei

Use the petals that have been separated from the crowns for this lei. Select those that are in the best condition and which have the smallest holes where the stems have been removed with the crowns.

It is sometimes best to use a strip of cloth or yarn to string this lei. A strip of cloth 1/4 to 1/2 inches in width will give greater uniformity if the holes in the petals are large. Because the petals are flat and compress easily, a minimum of 100 is recommended for this lei.

Step 1. Place several petals on the needle before transferring them to the string or cloth strip.

Step 2. Transfer the petals to the string or cloth strip and continue the process until a lei of petals of an appropriate length has been formed.

Step 3. Push the petals closely together and tie the ends of the string or cloth. Tie a bow at the point where the string ends have been tied to finish the lei.

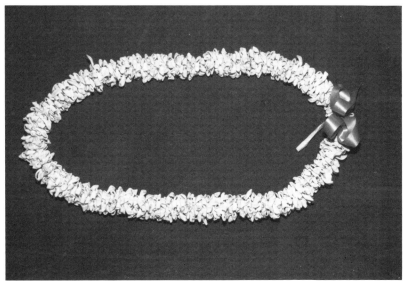

Crown Flower Buds

It will take from 60 to 80 buds to make a crown flower bud lei for normal use. If the lei is made with care, it takes on an appearance of a shell lei. Buds of approximately the same size should be selected for a uniform lei.

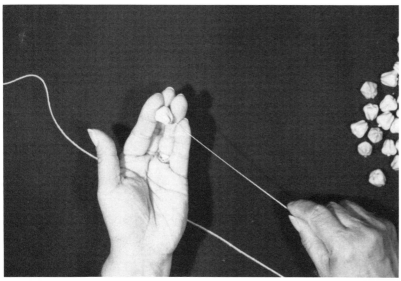

Step 1. Push the lei needle through the bud from the top end through the stem end.

Step 2. Because the bud is much more compact and solid than the flower, only 2 or 3 buds should be placed on the needle at a time. They are transferred to the string in the usual manner. Continue the process until a lei of appropriate length has been constructed.

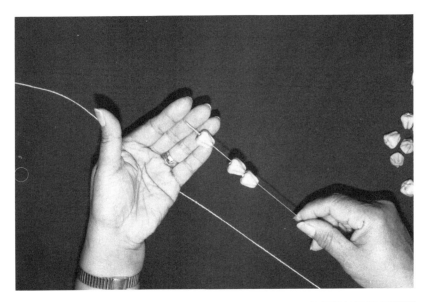

Step 3. Tie the ends of the string together, trim the loose ends, and tie a ribbon on the lei at the point where the string ends were tied to finish the lei.

Four different types of crown flower leis, whole crown flower lei, "crown" lei, crown flower bud lei, and a lei from the petals of the crown flower, are shown in this photograph.

Chapter 3

The *Lei Haku*

*T*he word *haku* has several meanings, as do many Hawaiian words. Used in describing a lei, the word means "to compose, put in order, arrange; to weave as a lei."[1] The *lei haku* is considered by many to be of Hawaiian origin and is referred to as the "traditional" Hawaiian lei, even though nontraditional flowers and foliage are used in its construction. Any method of mounting combinations of greenery, foliage, and flowers to a central backing material for the purpose of making an open-ended lei is commonly referred to as the *haku* style. Generally, the term includes the *lei humupapa* (sewn), sometimes called the *lei kuipapa* method; the *lei wili* (winding) method, and sometimes the *lei hili* (braided) method.[2] Traditional Hawaiian flower and foliage leis can also be braided *(hili),* wound *(wili),* or tied together by knotting *(hīpu'u)* the material making up the lei without the lei materials being mounted on any backing. However, if the method used in constructing the lei does not utilize backing material, technically, it would not be called a *lei haku.*

The most popular and common method of making the "traditional" Hawaiian lei is to mount selected flowers and other foliage, such as ferns, leaves, and multicolored foliage, on a natural base material. Dried banana leaves, ti leaves, and *lauhala* are common natural materials used as backing or undergirding for the outer parts of the lei. The floral components of the lei are secured to the base using raffia, *hau* fiber, No. 10 cotton string, or waxed thread.

Various types of *lei haku* are frequently used for the opening or dedication of buildings, roads, or public works projects. The *lei haku* must never be cut on these occasions but rather arranged so it may be easily untied and used as part of the decoration of the edifice during the ceremonies.

This chapter describes and illustrates two methods by which flowers and foliage are mounted or set against a base material. The first is properly termed the *lei wili* method, as string or raffia are used in securing the flowers and foliage to the various backing materials to provide firm support for the heavy lei. Constructing this type of lei allows the lei maker to develop a beautiful lei using any combination and assortment of flowers and foliage he or she finds to be the best expression of a par-

1. Mary Kawena Pukui, and Samuel H. Elbert, *Hawaiian Dictionary.*
2. Loraine E. Kuck, *The Story of the Lei.*

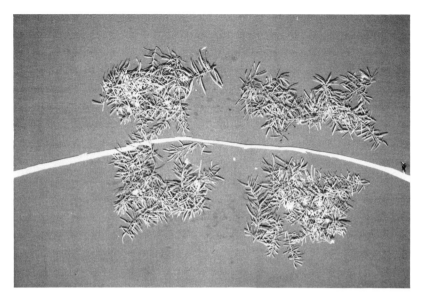

ticular design or pattern. The lei may be preplanned to incorporate specific materials or may simply be made with whatever materials are at hand. It is generally constructed as an open-ended lei. The length may vary and should be appropriate for the wearer's height. However, the lei should not be so heavy as to be uncomfortable for the wearer.

Shown here are the dried banana leaf, used for the lei's underbase, and asparagus fern *(Asparagus sprengeri).* The fern is used to cover the banana leaf base on which the flowers and foliage are attached. When the lei is viewed from the back, the binding should not be seen.

Another kind of foliage commonly used in the *lei haku* is leather fern *(Acrostichum).* It is generally imported from the mainland because of the short supply of the native *palapalai (Microlepia setosa)* fern. Leather fern is sturdy enough to protect the back of the lei and leafy enough to hide the base and raffia strands used in binding the foliage to the base. It also makes the lei more comfortable to wear.

LEI WILI METHOD *LEI HAKU*

Some of the blossoms used to make the *lei haku* described below were red baby roses, statice, both white and lavender, white mums, and yellow cushion mums. Baby's breath was also used. Although this blossom arrived in Hawaii quite recently, it is now common in many "traditional" Hawaiian leis. There are any number of other flowers and multicolored foliage that can be used in constructing *lei haku.*

Step 1. Select the natural base material on which the floral segments of the lei will be tied. The base component can be *lauhala,* ti leaf, dried banana leaf, *hau* bark, or even strips of *kapa* (bark cloth) or fabric. The material used to bind or *wili* the floral pieces to the base can be *hau* bark fiber, No. 10 cotton string, colored waxed carpet thread, or raffia. Raffia is used here for the binding and dried banana leaf for the backing.

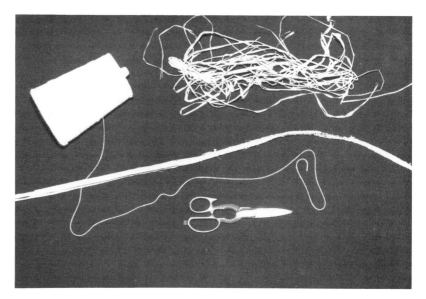

Step 2. Tie a slip knot in the end of the raffia. This knot should be placed about one inch from the end of the backing material to secure the raffia tightly to the base.

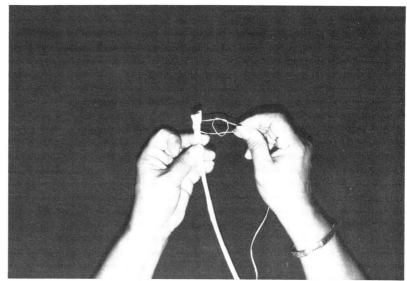

Step 3. Place two large pieces of asparagus fern at the end of the banana leaf and bind them tightly to the base, winding the raffia twice around the material.

Step 4. Then, winding the raffia around the fern and your forefinger (or middle finger), pass the end of the raffia through the opening between the finger and the banana leaf and pull it tight, removing the finger as the half-hitch becomes taut around the banana leaf. This half-hitch will securely anchor the beginning of the lei.

Step 5. Place two more pieces of fern on the base material and *wili* them. Make another half-hitch in the raffia to hold the fern in place.

Step 6. It is important that the front and the back of the lei be constructed at the same time, as the making of the lei proceeds. Turn the lei over so that the raffia binding attaching the fern to the banana leaf may be seen. Place a piece of leather fern on the back of the lei which will extend beyond the end of the banana leaf and also conceal the *wili* stitches.

Step 7. *Wili* the leather fern with two turns of the raffia. It is advisable, and necessary, to secure the work with a half-hitch in the binding material after every seven or eight turns; more often than that may cause the lei to become bulky and unmanageable.

Step 8. Place a second leaf of leather fern on the lei and *wili* the raffia around the leaf twice. Be sure to place and pull the raffia down in between the fern leaves so as to hide it from view.

Step 9. Turn the lei over with the front or flower side up and begin adding flowers. The first flowers must be tightly secured to the base material so that the *wili* raffia will hold the foliage and flowers added later; a half-hitch is advisable at this point.

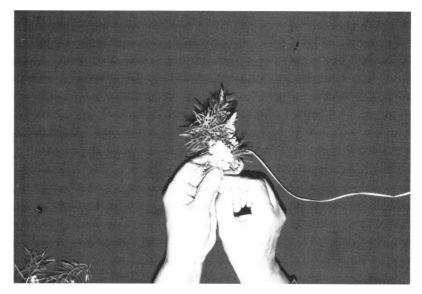

Step 10. After adding two or three flowers (one major blossom with smaller blossoms and baby's breath), turn the lei over and cover the wrapping material with two pieces of leather fern. The fern leaves should be bound to the lei one at a time.

Step 11. Go back to the front of the lei and begin adding flowers and greenery in an orderly way, tying them off with a half-hitch every seven or eight turns. It is best if your arrangement is preplanned. As your skill as a lei maker increases, this will be easier to do. Experienced lei makers work out a design or pattern beforehand, collect the necessary materials to carry out the design, and create works of art using the *wili* method for *lei haku.*

Step 12. Continue to add and *wili* flowers and greenery according to the plan, making sure that the flowers on the front and the fern on the back are added evenly for a smooth appearance. If the work must be left for a few minutes, simply tie a half-hitch and it will be secure until you return.

Step 13. Don't forget to secure the foliage by tying off the raffia after every seven or eight turns or as you think necessary.

Step 14. As more material is added to the lei, care should be taken to keep the arrangement of flowers and foliage making up the lei balanced and uniform. The design or pattern of flowers should develop as the lei progresses. Keep the width of the lei uniform as flowers and foliage are added. At any given time during the construction of the lei, the front and the back should be evenly wrapped and covered.

Remember that the back of the *lei haku* must be developed simultaneously with the front. As flowers are added to the front of the lei, fern leaves must be added to cover the back so that the raffia binding can't be seen.

COMPLETING THE LEI

There are at least two ways to complete a *lei haku* of this type, depending on personal preference, the skill of the lei maker, and the fragility of the flowers and other plants being used to make the lei. The lei maker may choose to *wili* from both ends and have the two parts meet in the center of the base strip. If so, the two ends are then brought together by binding flowers and foliage to the center of the open-ended lei, working from both directions, until they overlap.

When the lei is constructed this way, the fern leaves on the back point from the center out toward the ends of the lei. Working from both ends of the lei has a distinct disadvantage for the beginning lei maker. The lei must be turned many times in order to *wili* both sides at the same time. The novice lei maker is likely to damage the flowers on one end of the lei while turning and binding those on the other end. Working from one end of the base material to the other allows the lei maker to extend the unfinished end of the lei over the edge of the work table, thereby making it possible to complete the lei without turning it over again and again.

Step 15. When the lei has been completed to within 3 to 4 inches of the end of the base strip, tie a slip knot in another piece of raffia and place it on the dried banana leaf about 1 inch from the end of the base strip.

Step 16. Pull the slip knot tightly around the base strip. (This is the way the lei was begun at the other end.)

Step 17. Place a sprig of leather fern under the unfinished end with the fern pointing toward the end of the lei.

Step 18. Place two large sprigs of asparagus fern on the top side of the lei so that the end of the banana leaf is concealed and *wili* them securely to the base with the raffia.

Step 19. Add more fern leaves and wrap them tightly to the base.

Step 20. Turn the lei around so that the unfinished end is pointing away from you. This will allow you to examine the unfinished end and add more leather fern to the back of the lei if necessary without rolling the lei over.

Step 21. *Wili* blossoms and foliage to the base with the raffia until they meet and finally overlap the completed part of the lei. The material added to this end of the lei should match that on the other end in both kind and design.

The fern leaves will point in opposite directions, as shown here, and the tips of the fern will extend beyond the flowers at both ends. The fern must be added in such a way that it conceals the raffia binding.

Step 22. Once the two parts of the lei meet and overlap, bring the two ends of raffia together. Work them down into the floral material until they are concealed from view by holding the ends of the raffia tightly and moving them to and fro while pulling them toward the base material. Tie them securely together with the knot well below the surface of the foliage.

Step 23. Carefully clip the raffia ends closely to the knot and the lei is finished.

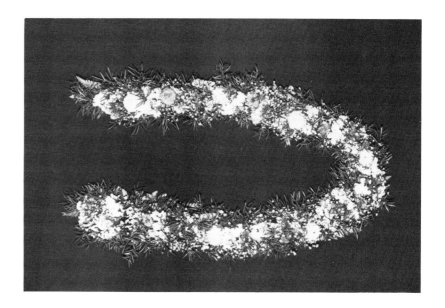

These two pictures show a completed *lei haku*. The first is a view of the front side and the second a view of the back. The appearance of the back of the lei is as important as that of the front. Anyone with a knowledge of *haku* leis will be certain to examine the back of the lei after viewing the front design.

LEI HAKU FOR THE HEAD

Lei haku are more commonly worn about the head or on hats than around the neck. *Lei haku* worn on the head or as a hat band are made using the same basic method as the full-length lei described above. The measurement for length should be taken by placing the base material around the head or hat. An allowance of about one-half a hat size or three-quarters of an inch should be made for the space taken up by the fern on the back of the lei. Fern leaves tied to the back of the lei will improve the wearing comfort of the lei on the head.

The head or hat lei should not be completely finished as with the full *lei haku*. The loose ends of string or raffia binding should be long enough to tie the lei together after a good fit has been determined.

HUMUPAPA STYLE *LEI HAKU*

The Hawaiians developed a method of lei making that facilitated the use of very delicate flowers such as pansies and ginger, as well as the flowers commonly used in other styles of leis. This style lei requires the use of a backing or foundation to which the flowers, ferns, and other material are sewn. The *lei humupapa* is generally used as a head or hat lei with *lauhala,* the outer skin of banana stock, or ti leaves as the backing material.

In making the lei, a large-sized sewing needle with an eye large enough to accommodate coarse threading material—raffia or thread—is needed. The floral materials may also be sewn to fabric or felt if a flexible backing is desired. The *humupapa* style has the advantage of allowing the lei maker to construct very wide leis such as those draped over the horses of *pā'ū* riders.

The front and back of the lei should be constructed at the same time; blossoms are sewn on the front side and the back is covered with fern or other foliage as the lei is constructed. The foundation or base to which the floral materials are sewn should not be visible when the lei is completed.

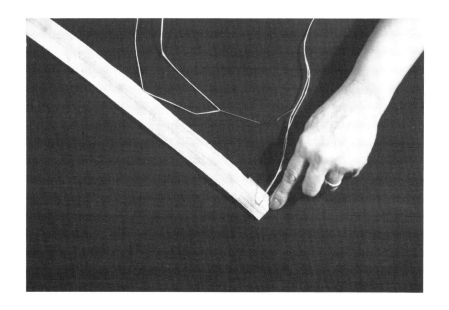

Step 1. Select your backing material (in this example, *lauhala* is used) and cut it to the desired width. Fold over a small section of about one and a half inches at the end to provide a solid base to hold the extra floral components at the end of the lei.

Step 2. Place various ferns, leaves, and flowers selected for the lei in the desired pattern as you begin. It is important that both sides of the lei be preplanned. The materials for the back of the lei should be positioned at the same time the materials for the front are put in place.

Step 3. Begin sewing the floral materials to the front of the base and the fern or other foliage to the back. As the stitches are pulled tight, care should be taken to conceal the thread (or raffia) by working it through the leaves, ferns, and flowers in such a way that it holds the different types of vegetation firmly by its main stems without hindering the movement of the leaves and flowers. The same stitches may be used to secure material to both sides of the base.

Step 4. Continue adding foliage and flowers to the backing, forming the preplanned design or pattern, and covering both sides as the lei develops.

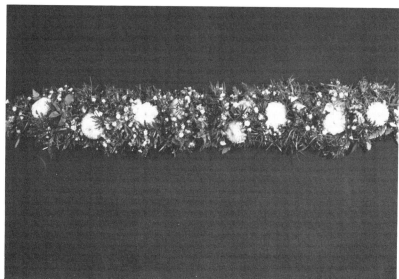

A typical finished *lei humupapa* will look something like the one pictured here.

This photo shows how the front and back sides of the lei completely cover the foundation material. The *humupapa* style *lei haku* has the advantage of holding its original shape when worn on a hat or the head. Long, narrow *humupapa* style leis may also be worn around the neck in the customary manner.

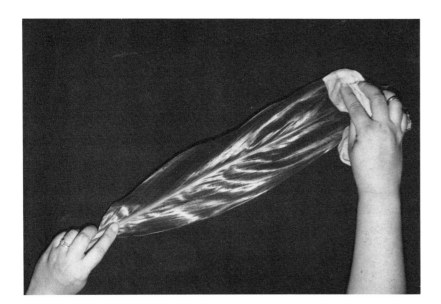

Step 1. Use a clean, damp cloth to wipe the leaves to remove any dirt and other unwanted materials.

Step 2. With a sharp pair of scissors, cut the leaf away from the midrib. One leaf will yield two pieces of usable leaf.

Here are the two pieces of leaf with the midrib removed which will be used in making the *wili* ti leaf lei.

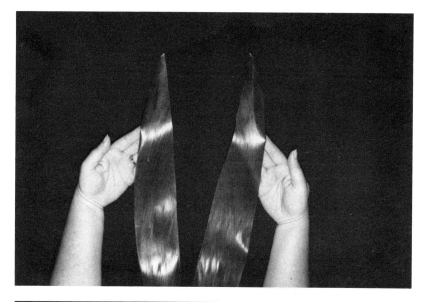

Step 3. Iron each leaf with an electric iron with the temperature set to about 150 degrees. If the iron is too hot, the leaf will be scorched and turn brown. If the iron is at the correct temperature the leaf surface will become shinier and the leaves will retain their flexibility. Leaves may also be prepared by dipping them in very hot water for a minute or two. Some lei makers place the ti leaves in the freezer for about 20 minutes to make them shiny. However, care should be taken not to freeze the leaves.

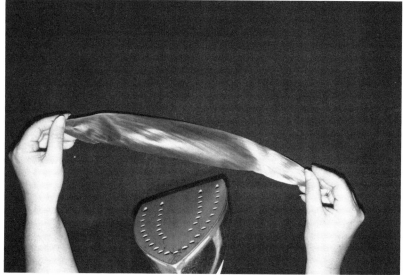

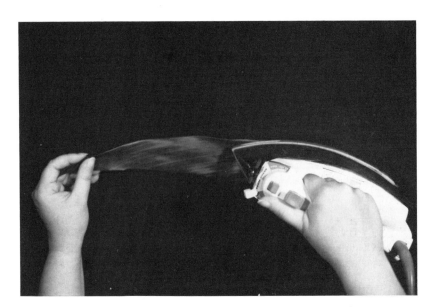

Step 4. Place the leaf half on the ironing surface with the shiny side up. Iron the leaf halves individually, leaving them smooth and shiny.

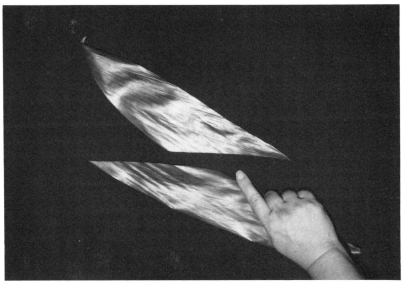

Step 5. Cut the ironed half leaves at a sharp angle (approximately 30 degrees) into two pieces, as shown here. The cut should produce sharp points on each half of the leaf, which will create decorative additions to the finished, cordlike lei.

Step 6. Take a quarter ti leaf in each hand, folding the points of each leaf. This will help you to twist *(wili)* the leaves into a lei.

Step 7. At this point, it is best to have another person assist in holding the tips of the leaves together as you begin the lei. Place the tip of the leaf held in the right hand under the tip of the leaf held in the left hand. Begin twisting each leaf tightly toward the right. After each leaf is twisted tightly for about 3 inches, *wili* the twisted leaves around each other, crossing the right hand over the left.

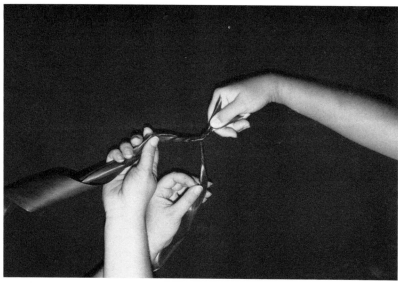

Step 8. After crossing the twisted leaves, change hands and continue to twist the leaves to the right to insure that the twisted leaves do not become unrolled and *wili* them together (always *right over left*). This combination of actions will form a strand of twisted and *wili* ti leaves.

Step 9. After you *wili* about 4 to 5 inches of the twisted leaves, tie a knot in the end of the ti leaf strand. The tips of the ti leaves which were crossed to begin the twisting should be left about $1\frac{1}{2}$ to 2 inches long. These tips will be used later in completing the lei.

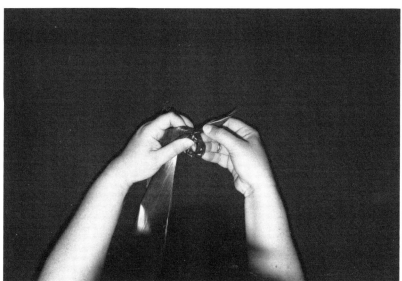

Step 10. After the knot has been securely tied, place it between the toes as shown here (or have another person hold it) in order to anchor the ti leaves and allow you to use both hands to twist and *wili* the leaves.

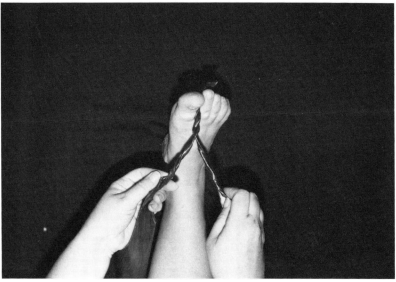

Step 11. Continue to twist the leaves to the right, *wili*, twist to the right, and *wili* the twisted leaves together, forming a single strand of ti leaves.

Step 12. When the pieces of leaves have been twisted to a point about 2 inches from the ends, add another piece of prepared ti leaf by splicing a new leaf onto each of the leaves making up the strand. Fold the tip of the new leaf and place it over the untwisted end of the leaf. About an inch or an inch and a half of the new leaf should be allowed to extend beyond the twisted parts of the ti leaf strand. Using an outward motion, roll the ends of the leaves together and make one twist.

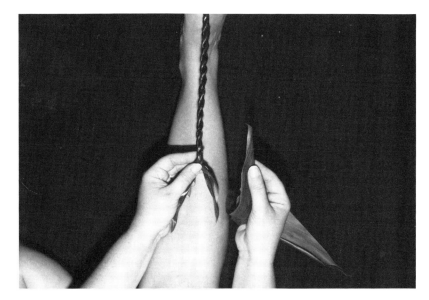

Step 13. Add another piece of ti leaf to the other part of the strand in the same way, twist the leaves together, and *wili* the lei.

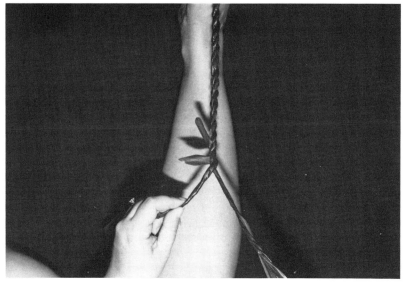

Step 14. Splice in other pieces of prepared ti leaf as necessary, leaving the tips exposed and free from the twisted strand. Continue this process until the strand reaches the desired length.

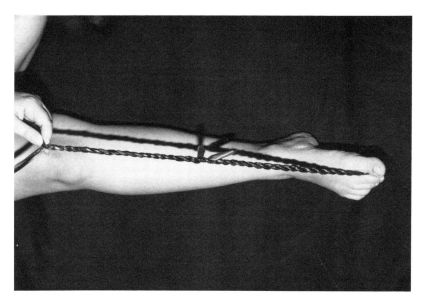

Step 15. When the strand is as long as you want it, tie a knot in the end of the strand with which you are working. Leave the loop of the knot open at this time.

Step 16. Pick up the opposite end of the strand (the end held between the toes) and push one of the extending tips of ti leaf through the loop of the knot.

Step 17. Pull the tip of the ti leaf through the loop in the knot.

Step 18. Pull the knot tightly closed.

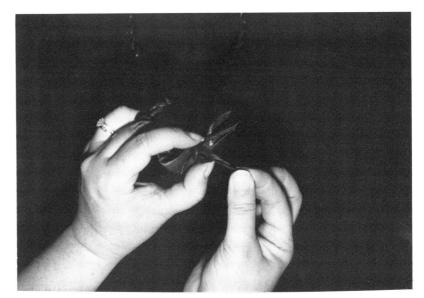

Step 19. Tie a square knot with the two loose tips of ti leaf. One tip should extend through the knot in the end of the strand and the other should remain outside. This completes a single strand ti leaf lei.

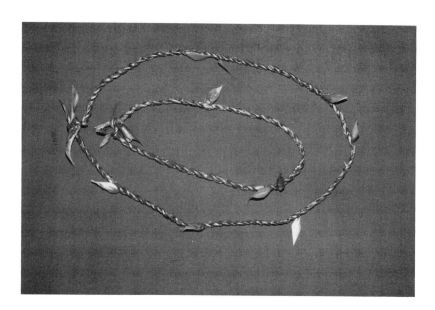

The pointed tips of the spliced leaves add a distinct beauty to the lei.

Strands of different lengths can be made to be worn together. It is also possible to braid *(hili)* three or more strands of this type of ti leaf lei together. Also, flowers may be added to the ti lei by placing them in the *wili* as the lei is constructed.

Chapter 4

The *Lei Wili*

*T*he *lei wili* is made by twisting or winding plant materials to form a lei. Two kinds of *lei wili* are demonstrated here: the ti leaf lei and the *maile* lei. The *maile* lei is also classified as a *hili* (braided) lei and sometimes a *hīpu'u* (knotted) lei.

THE TI LEAF LEI

Ti leaves *(lā'ī)* have always been important to the Hawaiian people and their way of life. A woody plant in the lily family, ti *(Cordyline terminalis)* was traditionally used for religious and ceremonial purposes as well as in everyday life in such practical ways as in the preparation of food, house thatching, and to make baskets, sandals, raincoats, and, more recently, hula skirts.

The ti leaf lei, a popular and long-lasting lei, is excellent for showing the *lei wili* method, since in this style of *wili,* the ti leaves must be both twisted and wound during the construction of the lei. This lei is made completely from ti leaves. For a single strand, select six to eight fresh, large ti leaves with no flaws.

Use large ti leaves without flaws to make the ti leaf lei.

THE *MAILE* LEI

Native Hawaiian *maile (Alyxia olivaeformis)* is a vinelike plant that grows among the trees in the forests of the lower and middle mountain regions, using their branches as a means of support. Hawaiian *maile* can be found throughout the state. The leaves of the shrub have a shiny, leathery appearance and are usually elliptical in shape and dark green in color. The bark and leaves grow loosely about a woody core, which makes it possible to strip the bark and leaves from the hard and inflexible shoots. When possible, mature shoots should be selected for leis, making the stripping of the bark easier. A distinct and pleasing fragrance is emitted by the bark and leaves, which enhances the desirability of the lei.

The *maile* lei is the traditional lei of Hawaii. *Maile* is known to have been used for leis by Hawaiians before the arrival of foreigners. The much-loved *maile* is also associated with Laka, the goddess of the hula.[3] Today *maile* leis are the favorite lei for many festive occasions; they are commonly worn or exchanged by the bride and groom at Hawaiian weddings, and victorious political campaigners celebrate with an assortment of leis, but the *maile* lei is always present. The *maile* lei is almost always presented to people opening a new business, with wishes of success. The dedication of a new building or highway demands the presence of *maile.*

Unfortunately, the true Hawaiian *maile* is becoming difficult to obtain and other varieties are being imported from the South Pacific to fill the demand. Sometimes the

3. Marie C. Neal, *In Gardens of Hawaii,* p. 690.

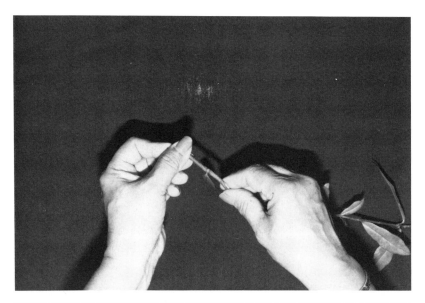

leaves of other plants or even trees, such as the Chinese banyan, are substituted for the *maile*. However similar their appearance, none of these substitutes has the unique fragrance of Hawaiian *maile*. As the demand for Hawaiian *maile* continues to grow, it is likely that enterprising persons will develop a way to cultivate and produce *maile* commercially.

Step 1. After the shoots have been gathered, while they are still fresh, strip the bark and leaves from the woody core. Break the bark loose from the core by grasping the shoot at the base end between thumb and fingers and twisting the bark around the core.

Step 2. As the bark begins to break loose, twist the bark for about 6 inches along the shoot, making sure the bark is free from the core.

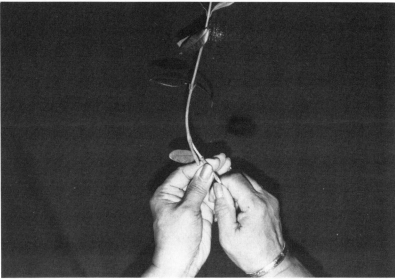

Step 3. Holding the base end of the shoot firmly with one hand, grasp the loose bark with the thumb and forefinger and slide the bark and leaves toward the tip of the shoot.

As the bark slides off the stem, it gathers or bunches, with the leaves remaining attached to the bark.

Step 4. Slide the bark along the core as far as possible. Usually the tips of the shoot will break away from the woody part of the core when the shoot becomes soft and pliable. If the core near the tip is flexible, it may be used as part of the lei.

Step 5. Break off the woody part of the core and discard it. Hold one end of the bunched bark and leaves in each hand and pull it to its full length. These lengths of bark and leaves are used to make the lei.

Step 6. Tie or splice together the sections to make a strand of *maile* as long as desired. Several lengths of *maile* are needed for one lei. The splicing can be accomplished by passing a leaf through a slit in the bark.

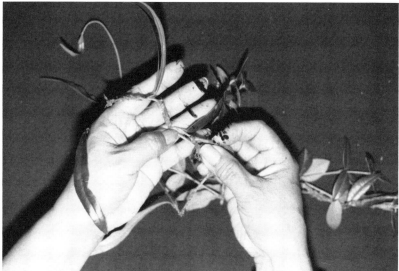

Here, the splicing is being done done by passing a leaf through a slit in the bark.

Here, sections of bark length are being tied together.

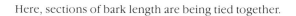

Here we see a finished single strand of waist-length *maile*.

Step 7. Once several lengths of *maile* have been spliced together into single strands, they are ready to be made into an attractive lei. Hold the strands of *maile* up with one hand and adjust them to approximately equal lengths.

Step 8. *Wili* (twist) the strands of *maile* together on one side of the lei and then on the other.

It is easier to hold the length of *maile* aloft with one hand while twisting the strands together with the other. If another person is present, he or she may assist in this operation.

Step 9. The lei is finished when you complete the *wili* of both sides. *Maile* leis are always open-ended and usually fall either to the waist or the knees after being draped over the shoulders.

The addition of a strand of *mokihana* enhances the *maile* lei both in appearance and fragrance, as the scent of the two plants complement one another. Sometimes strands of *pikake* or *'ilima* are twined about the *maile* to make beautiful and special leis.

Everyone delights in wearing a *maile* and *mokihana* combination lei.

Chapter 5

The *Lei Hīpuʻu*

*T*here are several Hawaiian plants which lend themselves to the *hīpuʻu* (knotted) style of lei making. *Lei hīpuʻu* are made by tying the stems of leaves or portions of vines together without the use of other material. The leaves of the *kukui* tree *(Aleurites moluccana)* as well as *ʻōlapa (Cheirodendron trigynum)* leaves are often knotted together to form leis with truly Hawaiian character. They have a unique beauty found only in a few native Hawaiian plants. When clusters of small white *kukui* blossoms are tied in with the light green leaves, the combination makes an attractive, distinctive lei. The red stems of the *ʻōlapa* contrasted with the brillant green color of its leaves create a rare and unusual natural lei.

Some types of ferns and a few vines can also be used in preparing *hīpuʻu* style leis. The fern leis are usually used by *hālau* (hula troupes) when conspicuous head and neck arrangements are desired. They may also be worn at the wrists and ankles.

To demonstrate the *lei hīpuʻu, kukui* leaves and blossoms will be used. This is only one of the methods for knotting leaves, but it will give the lei maker a basic knowledge of this type of lei.

Leaves of various sizes and clusters of blossoms grow at the ends of the *kukui* branches.

115

Step 1. Select the medium-sized leaves near the clusters of blossoms. Although any size leaves may be used, you should select leaves that are about the same size in order to have a uniform lei. Also, the stems of the medium size leaves are more pliable and can be knotted without breaking.

Step 2. The shiny side of the leaves should be facing out when the lei is worn. Break or cut the stems as long as possible.

Step 3. If you plan to tie clusters of blossoms in the lei, collect a sufficient number to provide a lei of uniform size and length.

Step 4. Tie a half-hitch knot in the stem of the first leaf. The knot should be far enough up the stem to keep them from becoming loose or untied.

Step 5. Pull the knot fairly tight, leaving the loop of the knot open enough to allow the stem of another leaf to pass through.

Step 6. Place the stem of the second leaf through the loop of the knot in the first leaf.

Step 7. Straighten the leaves so that they fall one on the other in a uniform manner.

Step 8. Tie a knot in the stem of the second leaf after the stem has passed through the loop of the first knot. A knot should be tied in the stem of each leaf. The size of the knot will prevent the leaf from slipping through the knot in the previous stem.

Step 9. Continue this process, building a series of leaves overlapping one another and held together by knots tied in the stems after they have been placed through the loop of each proceeding knot.

Step 10. If clusters of blossoms are to be added to the lei, the spacing should be predetermined and the stem of the blossom cluster placed in two loops and the knots pulled tightly. Care should be taken to avoid breaking the blossom cluster stem, as it is not as flexible as the leaf stem.

Step 11. Two separate groups of leaves and blossom clusters should be connected by tying and knotting the stems together. The groups of leaves should be uniform in length. Using the stem of the last leaf in each group, tie a square knot that will hold the two sides of the lei together. This completes the *lei hīpuʻu kukui*.

A cluster of blossoms may be added to the square knot to increase the beauty of the lei and also to disguise the knot that holds the two sides of the lei together.

From the back, the chainlike effect of the knots tied in each stem is easily visible.

This beautiful lei is worn draped over the shoulders.

APPENDIX 1

SUGGESTIONS FOR FLOWERS AND OTHER KINDS OF HAWAIIAN LEIS

There are many blossoms which can be used in making the single strand *(lei kui)*. Included in the list below are flowers common in Hawaii which can be easily obtained by the beginning lei maker. It is not intended to be a complete list of flowers that can be strung as a lei but simply a guide for selecting blossoms of different colors and characteristics that provide a variety of challenges for making leis. Therefore, only a relatively few flowers are listed for the beginning lei maker's use.

Flower Blossoms Commonly Used in Making the *Lei Pololei*

Carnation (different varieties)
Chrysanthemum (different varieties)
Crown flower
Hala (pandanus)
'Ilima
Gardenia
Ginger (yellow and white)
Globe amaranth *(leihua,* also *lehua mau loa* or *lehua pepa)*
Marigold
Mokihana

Pakalana (Chinese violet)
Pikake (jasmine)
Plumeria (*melia,* frangipani, many varieties)
Pua kenikeni
Rose *(lokelani)*
Stephanotis
Tuberose *(kupalo)*
Vanda orchid

Flower Blossoms Commonly Used in Making the *Lei Poepoe*

'Ākulikuli
Bougainvillea
Carnation (different varieties)
Chrysanthemum (different varieties)
Crown flower
Gardenia
Globe amaranth
Kika (cigar flower)
Pakalana
Pikake
Plumeria, many varieties
Pua kenikeni
Tuberose

Other Kinds of Hawaiian Leis

There are many other leis which can be constructed when flowers are not available. These artificial leis can be used to give a Hawaiian greeting or produce an aloha atmosphere at parties, social gatherings, or other special occasions.

As mentioned previously, leis can be made from almost anything. A few ideas for materials and styles which can be used in making an attractive lei are presented below.

Crepe Paper: The process for manufacturing crepe paper was developed in 1897. It immediately became very popular for decorating everything from dance halls and grandstands to bulletin boards and school rooms. Many other decorative uses were found for this wonderful crinkled paper. At the turn of the century and through the years of World War II, crepe paper leis were used to a much greater extent than floral leis in Hawaii. These leis are still worn on special occasions.

To make a lei, cut the crepe paper in strips about 1 inch wide and sew the strips lengthwise with a running stitch. By twisting and compressing the threaded strips, colorful and useful leis can be made rather quickly. About fifteen to twenty strips of crepe paper will be required for each lei.

Fabric: One-inch wide strips of various colored fabric can be used to make very attractive leis. The vertical threads of the fabric are individually removed along the edge of each strip. When the threads have been removed from both edges and only about a $1/4$ to $1/2$ inch strip of fabric remains, the fabric can be sewn with a running stitch much the same as with the crepe paper lei. When a strip of fabric has been stitched about 6 to 10 inches, the fabric is twisted and compressed, making a *poepoe* type lei. About ten to fifteen 6 to 10 inch strips of fabric are necessary to make a single lei. The fabric lei has a velvetlike texture, making it very pleasant to wear. This type lei will last as long as the dye in the material retains its color.

Yarn: Attractive leis may be made by wrapping yarn around drinking straws. Three or more straws can be used at the same time, provided the wrapping proceeds uniformly up the straws. The object is to pass the ends of two or three lengths of yarn which have been cut to the desired length through the straw(s). These lengths of yarn are secured with a safety pin or by tying them in a knot. Another length of yarn is then wrapped around the drinking straw, creating many circles or loops of yarn. The yarn is pushed off the end of the straws as they become encircled with yarn. The lengths of yarn inside the straw will support the circles of yarn as the loops grow in length. At the end, the loops and inside lengths of yarn are tied together with a ribbon affixed at the point where the knots appear. If this lei is done with yellow or orange yarn, it appears similar to an *'ilima* lei from a distance.

It is also possible to *wili* two lengths of rick-rack braid into an attractive lei. Although this lei does not resemble any flower lei it can be made quickly when a lei is needed in a hurry.

Money: There are several ways to make leis from currency or coins. If coins are to be used, each coin is wrapped in square pieces of cellophane. The ends of the cellophane are secured with transparent tape, rubber bands, or string to hold the coins securely. The wrapped coins are then tied into a lei with short pieces of string or ribbon.

Currency leis can be made by folding the bill lengthwise, tying the bill in the center and pulling the ends of the folded bill out to form a flower effect. A length of string can be used to hold the currency in a lei configuration.

Gum, candy, or cracked seeds: Leis made from packs of gum, pieces of candy wrapped in cellophane are always a welcome treat for children. Island children enjoy leis made with packages of Chinese cracked seed. The lei is constructed by wrapping each package in cellophane and tying the cellophane wrappers together. About thirty packages are needed to make a lei of appropriate length.

APPENDIX 2

CARE OF FLOWERS AND LEIS

Generally, blossoms will last longer when they are picked in the early hours of the morning—even before sunrise. Refrigeration extends the useful life of the blossoms and keeps them in good condition for use in constructing leis. Most blossoms can be stored dry and in a plastic bag at about 36 degrees Fahrenheit; others, such as *pua kenikeni,* will keep best in a flat container between two damp paper towels in a dark place. The vanda orchid must not be moistened before being placed in the refrigerator, as the moisture will cause the color of the petals to fade.

There are a number of ways to care for blossoms once they have been constructed into a lei. Commercial lei makers usually hang the finished leis in refrigerated showcases. When a lei is purchased they place it in a plastic bag. The bag is held at the open end with both hands and pulled partly shut. It is then whirled two or three times in such a way as to trap as much air as possible inside the bag. The twisted ends of the plastic bag are tied together to close the bag. This cushions the flowers and gives the lei as much air as possible for "breathing." Of course, the bag should be kept in a cool place and never placed in direct sunlight.

More recently commercial lei makers have been placing one or more pieces of ti leaf in the bottom and along the sides of the plastic bag. *Lā ʻī* (ti leaf) has been used by the Hawaiians for many years, long before refrigeration was introduced to the islands, in connection with keeping flowers fresh. The ti leaves provide moist air inside the plastic bag and, to some degree, keep the temperature constant. The delicate blossoms of certain leis have been known to "burn" or wither more quickly than normal when they are in contact with the plastic.

Carnation leis will last longer if they are submerged in lukewarm water, the excess water shaken off, and placed in a plastic bag for storage at about 36 degrees. They can also be preserved for a day or two by simply placing them in a plastic bag, sealing the bag with as much air as the bag will hold, and putting it in the refrigerator.

Pūʻolo lā ʻī (A bag made from ti leaves)

Many years ago, Hawaiians learned to make ti leaf bags or containers for carrying fruits, vegetables, and other food products found in the forest and mountains of the islands. When the flower lei became popular, the *pūʻolo lā ʻī* was adapted for carrying and preserving leis. To this day, the *pūʻolo lā ʻī* is the best way to keep and transport

flower leis. The moisture provided naturally by the ti leaf and the insulation created by layers of leaves tied together keep the flowers moist and cool. In addition, a lei maker who carries leis in one or more *pū'olo lā'ī* adds a sense of authenticity to the entire work.

There are at least two ways to construct an effective *pū'olo lā'ī*. Both methods will be shown.

Pū'olo lā'ī with stem

Step 1. Perhaps the fastest and most sturdy *pū'olo lā'ī* is made by breaking or cutting the stem of the ti plant approximately 6 to 8 inches below the lowest leaves on the upright plant. This section of woody stem will later be used as a handle.

Step 2. Place the ti plant with all the leaves attached upside down on a smooth, hard surface. Spread the leaves evenly, with the section of woody stem held vertically. Tie the stem ends of the leaves tightly together about 4 to 6 inches below the woody stem of the plant using half of a dried ti leaf that has been soaked in water to make it pliable and strong.

Step 3. Place the lei or leis to be transported loosely around the woody stem of the plant.

Step 4. While holding the woody stem in one hand, begin pulling the leaves by their ends up to the woody stem. Each leaf should overlap the next leaf to be drawn up to the stem leaving room enough to hold the lei(s) firmly without folding or bending the petals of the blossoms.

Step 5. Gather the ends of the ti leaves about the woody stem and tie them tightly using dried ti leaf that is wet or the stem end of a large ti leaf.

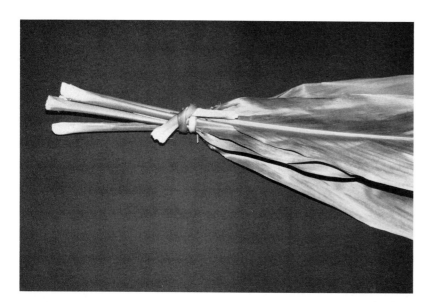

Pū'olo lā'ī with individual leaves

Step 1. Select a dozen or more ti leaves and remove them from the stock of the ti plant.

Step 2. Place the leaves in a circle on a flat surface with the midrib side of the leaves facing up. Gather the stem ends of the leaves together, while the leaves remain flat on the surface.

Step 3. Using a dampened, dried ti leaf or strong cord, tie the stem ends of the leaves together. The leaves should form a circle on the working surface.

Step 4. Place the lei to be stored or transported over the stem ends of the ti leaves and begin pulling the ends of the leaves up to the stem ends. The leaves should overlap one another and form a storage pouch for the lei.

Step 5. After all the ends of the ti leaves have been gathered around the stem ends, tie them firmly together using a strong cord, dried ti leaf, or a midrib removed from a large ti leaf. (By removing the midribs from each leaf before forming the *pū'olo lā'ī* you can make a softer, more flexible storage pouch for the leis.)

Banana Stalk Lei Carrier *(Hā mai'a)*

Sections of banana stalk make perfect, natural trays for storing and transporting open-ended leis—especially the *haku* style lei. Cut a banana tree close to the ground with a sharp machete or axe, measure the banana stock to the desired length, and cut it cleanly at that point. Banana stalks grow in layers that are half the circumference of the stalk and which overlap at the edges.

Peel away the outer layers and select one the proper size to accommodate the lei to be carried. Place the lei in the banana tray for storage and transportation. The banana stalk is naturally moist, keeping the lei straight and firmly supported. Care should be taken when working with fresh banana stalk as the juice draining from the stalk will permanently stain clothing.

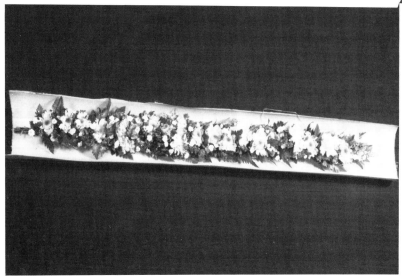

SELECTED BIBLIOGRAPHY

Bird, Adren J, Steven Goldsberry, and J. Puninani Kanekoa Bird. *The Craft of Hawaiian Lauhala Weaving.* Honolulu: University of Hawaii Press, 1982.

Brown, Elizabeth D. W. "Polynesian Leis." *American Anthropologist* 33, no. 4 (October–December), 1931.

Kuck, Loraine E. *The Story of the Lei.* Honolulu: Tongg Publishing Co., 1983.

Law, Napua, and Sharman Francisco. *Hawaiian Flower Leis.* Laie, Hi.: Brigham Young University, Institute for Polynesian Studies, 1979.

Learsi, Rufus. *Israel: A History of the Jewish People.* Cleveland: World Publishing Co., 1947.

McDonald, Marie A. *Ka Lei: The Leis of Hawaii.* Honolulu: Topgallant Publishing Co., 1978.

Moscati, Sabatino. *The Face of the Ancient Orient.* Chicago: Quadrangle Books, 1963.

Neal, Marie C. *In Gardens of Hawaii.* Bernice P. Bishop Museum Special Publication 50. Honolulu: Bishop Museum Press, 1965.

Pukui, Mary Kawena, and Samuel H. Elbert. *Hawaiian Dictionary.* Revised and Enlarged Edition. Honolulu: University of Hawaii Press, 1986.

Watson, Don. *Plants are for People.* Honolulu: Hawaiian Service, Inc., 1973.

ABOUT THE AUTHORS

Adren J Bird is associate professor of education at Brigham Young University, Hawaii Campus. He first came to Hawaii in 1947. On Maui, he met the Kanekoa family, who gave him a love and appreciation of the Hawaiian way of life. He has endeavored to learn, understand, teach, and help preserve the various aspects and values of the Hawaiian culture from that time on. Since 1973, he has worked with most of the high schools on Oahu on various teacher training programs. The improvement of Hawaii's public schools through the training of better qualified teachers holds a high priority in his goals for the future. Photography has been a hobby of his since high school days. He put it to good use in producing this book and *The Craft of Hawaiian Lauhala Weaving,* co-authored with Steven Goldsberry and J. Puninani Kanekoa Bird.

Josephine Puninani Kanekoa Bird was born in Hana, Maui, and raised in Nahiku in an extended family setting. She learned Hawaiian crafts and culture at a very young age from her grandmother, mother, aunties, and uncles. She has taught many courses in Hawaiian crafts over the years, among them lauhala weaving and feather lei making both at the Polynesian Cultural Center in Laie and while living on the mainland. She has been a member of the May Day court and participated in the annual Kamehameha Day parade as a *pāʻū* rider for three years. She was honored by being selected as *moʻi wahine* by the Polynesian Cultural Center when the crew of the voyaging canoe *Hōkūleʻa* was honored following their first and second voyages. She is co-author of *The Craft of Hawaiian Lauhala Weaving.*